HISTORY

COURSEWORK COMPANION

Martin Parsons

GCSE

Charles Letts & Co Ltd
London, Edinburgh & New York

First published 1989
by Charles Letts & Co Ltd
Diary House, Borough Road, London SE1 1DW

Text: © Martin Parsons 1989
Illustrations: © Charles Letts & Co Ltd 1989
Cover photograph: Tim Moore
Handwriting samples: Artistic License
Illustrations: Peter McClure

British Library Cataloguing in Publication Data

Parsons, Martin
    GCSE history. – (Letts coursework companion)
    1. History
    I. Title
    900

ISBN 0 85097 861 0

Acknowledgements
The author and publisher wish to thank the
following for permission to use photographs and
cartoons for which they hold the copyright:
British Film Institute, p. 31 (top); Imperial
War Museum, p. 15, 16, 31 (bottom), 78, 79, 80;
The Mansell Collection Ltd, p. 29; Mary Evans
Picture Library, p. 77 (bottom); University of
Kent, p. 25

Printed and bound in Great Britain by
Charles Letts (Scotland) Ltd

Contents

Introduction

The introduction of GCSE courses has provided students of history in schools with the opportunity to demonstrate their ability as historians and not just be passive receivers of facts given to them by their teachers or gathered from books.

Coursework is an extremely important part of all examination groups' syllabuses and although criteria and requirements may differ, the actual methods of dealing with coursework remain basically the same.

In this book we shall examine the skills required to obtain the best marks from a 'coursework assignment' carried out in the classroom and for homework and briefly consider the requirements for individual studies.

All the skills and methods highlighted in this book can be adapted to suit the needs of your study and the requirements of the major examination groups.

During the course of this book you will consider the skills of careful observation and interpretation of classroom material, as well as basic research techniques required for an individual study. You will also find examples of actual coursework assignments, with an indication of how marks can be awarded.

Remember that these skills are not only useful for passing the GCSE examination. It is hoped that you will enjoy being a research historian and develop your skills to the point where you can begin to pose your own questions and theories about historical data, and maintain an interest in the subject long after the examination has been passed!

NB The GCSE syllabuses of some of the groups are still being refined and changes are being made. It is, therefore, **very important** that throughout the course your seek the advice of your teacher.

I am greatly indebted to James McInnes, Head of History at The Emmbrook School, Wokingham, for his constructive criticism and advice throughout the project. Also my thanks to Philip Hull, Head of History at Theale Green School, for allowing me to use examples of coursework assignments; and to my wife and daughters for their continued understanding and support.

Martin Parsons, 1989

What is coursework?

All GCSE examination groups will require candidates to do coursework. This may take several forms and may involve a number of pieces of work set by the teacher on various topics, some of them completed outside the classroom for homework. It could include a lengthy individual study. It could also be a combination of these. At least 20 per cent of your final examination grade will be based on this coursework.

Each examination group will place a different emphasis on the marks available for coursework. The **history criteria** has set a minimum level of 20 per cent but there is no upper limit; so, in theory, the final grade could be based **entirely** on coursework. In practice this is **not** the case and most groups have set a level of between 20 and 40 per cent. Whatever the proportion of marks they allocate to this section of the syllabus, poor coursework can make a significant difference to the **overall grade** of a candidate. Therefore it will be a very important part of your history study and you should put a lot of effort into gaining as many marks as possible for your coursework.

> *It is very important to ask your teacher about any aspect of your coursework.*

GCSE provides the ideal opportunity for those students who find it difficult to sit formal examinations to **raise** their overall grade by working hard **in their own time**. It can be a little more difficult to do well in classroom assignments where sometimes there is a set time limit, but here, usually, the teacher will allow time for preparation and this will help if you are conscientious.

All examination groups have published details about the way in which coursework is to be organized. They have laid down the objectives which need to be assessed and therefore have indicated the sort of work they believe the classroom teacher needs to set in order to achieve the overall aims of the course of study.

NB Your school may be following a **Schools History Project** course. The details of this course can be found in the Appendix. It is worth remembering that the skills, aims and objectives of this course are similar to those of GCSE. However, the marking, assessment and percentage allocated to coursework differ, so Sections Three and Four, dealing with the levels of response in GCSE, are not necessarily relevant to a Schools History Project.

Your teacher will know the requirements for the examination you are taking. You must always listen very carefully to what your teacher has to say in order to achieve the best results. If you do not understand what you need to do **you must ask**.

Remember, coursework is not just some ordinary piece of work that you can take lightheartedly. It is very important and although you may be writing it 18 months before the final examination and it might seem to you to be just another piece of classwork it could make a difference to your overall GCSE grade.

There are too many groups to provide detailed information about coursework criteria for all of them. However, there are similarities and the notes on the examples of actual requirements shown on the chart in the Appendix, together with a detailed written explanation, should give you some indication of what is required as well as perhaps highlighting the demands of your particular group.

Assessment objectives

The **assessment objectives** referred to in the chart in the Appendix can be broadly defined as follows. (Remember there will be slight differences in interpretation and the description of these objectives by individual examination groups.)

(a) Selection, deployment and communication of historical knowledge:
- to select and evaluate knowledge which is relevant to the context
- to analyse and synthesize such knowledge
- to display and deploy it in a clear, concise and coherent form.

(b) The use of analytical/basic concepts; to make use of and understand the concepts of:
- cause and consequence
- continuity and change
- similarity and difference.

(c) Look at events and issues from the perspective of people in the past (empathy). (See Section Five for a detailed interpretation of Empathy.)

(d) Use of evidence:
To show the skills necessary to study a wide variety of historical sources such as Primary and Secondary written sources, statistical and visual material, artefacts, textbooks and orally transmitted material.

These skills can be displayed by:
- showing an understanding of the evidence and extracting relevant information from it
- interpreting and evaluating it, thereby distinguishing between fact, opinion and judgment; highlighting the shortcomings of the evidence such as inconsistencies and gaps; detecting bias
- comparing various types of evidence and reaching conclusions based on these sources.

(These skills can all be displayed in a local study as well as classroom assignments.)

The organization of coursework

In the Appendix you can see the coursework requirements of all the major examination groups. You should note that there are similarities in the actual historical skills they want to test. However, the way in which coursework can be presented, the number of assignments required, the maximum number of words acceptable and the percentage of marks made up by coursework content vary considerably from group to group.

Your history teacher will give you all these details at the beginning of your course, or perhaps even earlier, when you are about to choose your options. You will be told the name of the examination group you will be entered for and the actual syllabus you will be taking, if there is a choice. Your teacher should also tell you the coursework requirements for the syllabus. This is **very important information**. If you are not given a handout containing the details make sure you copy the relevant facts down from what you are told and keep them in a safe place for reference.

If you have any questions about your course, no matter how simple, this is the time to ask your teacher. It would be useful, for instance, if you had a **broad idea** of the whole course. If the teacher only outlines the coursework needed for, say, a term or one year ask where it fits into the overall pattern. **Remember**, history will not be the **only** subject you take at GCSE requiring coursework, so if you can see the overall course it might help you to see where the busy times will be during the following two years.

There should be a number of questions which you can ask yourself or your teacher. The list below might highlight some of these questions but it is not a complete list and there may be many others that you need to ask in order to sort out a particular problem.

- Which examination group will I be entered with?
- Which syllabus am I taking?
- How many assignments do I have to do?
- When do I have to hand in the assignments?
- Are all these assignments to be done in class or do I have to do an individual study?
- Is there any limit to the number of words I can use and, if so, what is it?
- What happens if I miss an assignment?
- Do all my assignments have to be in written form?

The first two questions can be answered by your teacher quite easily. Once you have this information the subsequent questions become easier to answer as well. The number of assignments you have to complete is stipulated by the group and although in some cases you are given some lee-way (e.g. the NEA syllabus 'A' requires between four and seven assignments), they are generally an **immovable** demand. However, you will probably be asked to do **more** than the minimum of coursework assignments. This will work to your advantage because the teacher may then select the **two** assignments for which you obtained the highest marks as a basis for your final coursework grade. Whether you are able to do these assignments in school or at home will depend on your teacher.

You may have the option of doing an **individual study** which will be completed in your own time outside school (Section Six covers this), but generally assignments will be done in the classroom with perhaps the possibility of completing them for homework. The **word limit** on these assignments is very important and you should keep a check on the number of words you use. If the word limit is 1500 then work to this total. You should not be penalized by your teacher if you go over **slightly**, but 1500 does not mean 2000, or even 1750 words! Do not worry too much if the number of words you have used is below that expected by the group, but make sure your answers satisfy the coursework objectives! They do not weigh the coursework and they are more interested in quality rather than quantity.

The question of time allowed for coursework is difficult to answer here because it will be the responsibility of individual schools to deal with the collection of coursework. In theory there should be no time limit for the completion of work. In practice there probably **will** be deadlines for the completion of coursework, especially where a number of pieces are being set, so that the teacher can mark the work and provide feedback before the next task. You probably will not be told the actual marks you have gained but your teacher might well give you a general indication of levels. You need to check timings with your own teacher.

Each examination group has set a date by which coursework has to be sent to the **coursework moderators**, who then have to check that the marking and levels of attainment are correct. In most cases your teachers will have to read and mark all of the work first.

Some schools may give you extra time in order for you to meet the requirements and complete a coursework file; other schools may not, and therefore may penalize you by reducing the number of marks available for the piece of work. For some groups this can be quite a sizeable percentage and could easily mean a difference of more than one grade at the end of the course! If you miss coursework for genuine reasons, for example illness, the group will usually accept a **medical certificate** as evidence and, possibly, give you a grade for the missing work based on your other assignments. So if you are away for a genuine reason, don't panic!

Some groups, such as NEA and LEAG, allow candidates to submit work in non-written form. This could mean the making of a model, work on audio-tape (e.g. an interview with somebody), or a collection of photographic evidence or film. However, this form of coursework cannot be handed in on its own. It **must** be accompanied by a written explanation which should refer to its significance as a piece of coursework, i.e. how it meets the requirements set by the teacher, how it was made or carried out and the conclusions you draw from it. This particular aspect of coursework is covered in Section Ten. Before you attempt anything like this it is essential that you discuss your ideas with your teacher to make sure your work complies with the group's requirements.

Finally, a word of advice on time management. When you start an external examination course at the beginning of the fourth year, you can see two years ahead, and there is often a tendency to believe that there is plenty of time. But beware! There will be other demands on your time. Assignments for different subjects may be due in on the same day. There may be time limits for handing in coursework. You may have to do individual studies in more than one subject. If you don't look at **all** of your GCSE exams in broad terms you could find yourself having to catch up with a lot of work at the last minute. The simplest thing to do is to organize your time, not forgetting to make allowances for your interests outside school. Try to find out when assignments will be required for all your subjects and plot them on a two-year planner, which you can make up for yourself, going from the September of your fourth year to the July of your fifth.

If you cannot get the information straight away, add it to the chart as and when it becomes available. In this way you will see at a glance any 'pressure-points' which might occur and you should be able to plan your time accordingly to avoid any panic. Remember, if you are doing an individual study, do not forget to leave yourself time for a holiday! Do not spend **all** your summer or Easter break working!

Checklist

1 Make sure you have a copy of your examination group's requirements.

2 Do not be afraid to ask questions about the course in general at the beginning.

3 There are a number of specific questions that need to be asked of yourself and your teacher. Examples of such questions are listed on page 7, but remember it is not a complete list.

4 Take particular note of time and word limits.

5 Take advice from your teacher before starting any non-written coursework or individual study.

6 If you miss a piece of coursework because of illness obtain a medical certificate.

7 Make up a time management chart and plot the assignment dates for *all* your subjects; highlight pressure points.

Year Planners

1990	Monday	Tuesday	Wednesday	Thursday	Friday	Saturday	Sunday
September 3							
10	G C S E COURSES START						
17							
24							
October 1							
8							
15	←		HALF TERM				→
22							
29							
November 5							
12			ASSIGN DUE (H)		ENG. ASSIGN.		
19							
26							
December 3					GEOG. ASSIGN.		
10							
17							
24	/	/	C / H R / I S / T M / A S / / /				
31	/	/	H / O L / I D / A / Y /				
1991 **January** 7	TERM STARTS						
14							
21							
28							
February 4							
11							
18	←		HALF TERM				→
25							
March 4							
11		C.D.T.					
18							
25							
April 1							
8	/	/ E / A S / T E / R / H O / L / I / D / A Y /					
15							
22	TERM STARTS						
29							
May 6							
13							
20							
27							
June 3	←		HALF TERM				→
10							
17					GEOG. ASSIGN.		
24							

	Monday	Tuesday	Wednesday	Thursday	Friday	Saturday	Sunday
July	1						
	8						
	15						
	22						
	29						
August	5	*S*	*U*	*M*	*M*	*E*	*R*
	12	*H*	*O*	*L*	*I*	*D*	*A* *Y* *S*
	19						
	26						
September	2 *TERM STARTS*						
	9						
	16 *C.D.T.*						
	23						
	30						
October	7						
	14						
	21	←		*HALF*	*TERM*		→
	28						
November	4						
	11		*ASSIGN DUE (H)*		*ASSIGN DUE (ENG)*		
	18						
	25						
December	2						
	9						
	16						
	23		*C* *H*	*R* *I*	*S* *T*	*M* *A*	*S*
	30						
1992 **January**	6 *TERM STARTS*						
	13	←		*MOCK*	*EXAMS*		→
	20						
	27						
February	3						
	10						
	17	←		*HALF*	*TERM*		→
	24						
March	2						
	9		*HISTORY ASSIGN.*				
	16						
	23						
	30						
April	6		*E* *A*	*S*	*T* *E*	*R*	
	13		*H* *O*	*L*	*I* *D*	*A* *Y*	
	20						
	27		*END OF COURSEWORK*				
May	4						
	11						
	18						
	25						

Fig. 2.1 A two-year planner

Coursework assignments

As you may have already seen in the Appendix, coursework marks make a significant contribution to the final GCSE grade. It makes sense that any coursework assignments set must be taken seriously whether they are completed at home or in class. At various times during the course, usually at the end of a particular topic, you will be given an assignment by your teacher which will test one or more of the **assessment objectives** laid down in the syllabus for your exam. As we have already seen, these objectives may differ slightly in meaning, or in written form, from one group to another but they all require similar responses.

Your teacher will usually write your assignment using material relevant to the topic you are studying at the time so you should have some background knowledge before you are given it. The questions will be set in such a way that all candidates are able to carry out the tasks and assignments set, using appropriate skills at their own individual levels of ability.

Coursework marks will be awarded for positive achievement.

In most cases your completed assignments will be marked by your own teacher or a member of the History department in your school.

The teacher will have to construct a **mark scheme** on which to base the allocation of marks for specific types of answers. The mark scheme used by the teacher will reward **positive** achievement. In other words, you will be given credit for what you **know** rather than be marked down for what you do **not** know!

Having organized a mark scheme based on the **level of response** to be expected from candidates at the various levels of historical understanding or **levels of empathetic awareness**, your teacher will allocate marks for different qualities of answer. Again this will depend on the requirements of the group but generally the objectives mentioned below will be taken into consideration, and credit will be given for those answers which fulfil the objective being assessed. Your teacher may also give credit within the **levels** for other qualities such as:

- the use of precise accurate material
- the use of brief, relevant quotations
- your ability to argue a point
- evidence of your own ideas and views
- your ability to use historical concepts.

The exact mark scheme will depend on the tasks undertaken during a particular assignment and so the marks available can change each time depending on the objectives being tested by a particular assignment.

It is assumed by the examination groups that during the two year course students will attempt a number of assignments. It is then permissible for the teacher to choose the best ones for submission for the final grade. For example if you are doing SEG you will only need to submit two pieces of coursework so you may be able to choose the best two from a much larger number you completed throughout the course. Remember, though, that these must include the best **empathy** assignment, the best **document** exercise, the best **factual knowledge** assignment etc. You will **not** be allowed to submit just the best ones overall.

Assignments must be your own work.

It is very important to remember that all pieces of coursework should be **your own original work**. You may be able to get some advice from your teacher, who may be able to suggest some background reading or other information which may be relevant, or discuss any problems you might have with understanding specific tasks, or even give advice on the correct way to write assignments. Your teacher will **not** be able to provide you with detailed notes specifically concerned with the assignment in

Ability	Grade F	Grade C
	In order to be awarded **Grade F**, a candidate will be expected to:	In order to be awarded **Grade C**, a candidate will be expected to:
In relation to knowledge	**(a)** display a limited amount of accurate and relevant historical knowledge; show a basic understanding of the historical concepts of **cause and consequence**, **continuity** and **change**, (all supported by simple examples) and to identify difference and similarity.	**(a)** use relevant historical knowledge as accurately as possible to support a logical argument; distinguish between the cause and occasion of an event and to show some ability to analyse historical problems; demonstrate that changes in history do not necessarily take place in a 'linear' or 'progressive' way (i.e. straight after one another in a continual sequence), to contrast people, events, issues and institutions.
In relation to understanding and values	**(b)** show occasional understanding of why and how people in the past acted as they did. **(c)** show ability to understand basic evidence and to extract partial and/or general information from it.	**(b)** demonstrate some understanding of historical concepts, to appreciate that many of them are complex and to use appropriate evidence. **(c)** show the ability to look at events from the perspective of people in the past; understand the importance of searching for motives; display imagination in seeing the past through the eyes of the people living at the time. **(d)** show an understanding of a number of sources either by analysis of statistical data or summarizing information given in a document; answer accurately questions requiring specific information to be extracted from the sources.
In relation to skills	**(d)** show the obvious limitations of a particular source of information and to list some of the sources needed to reconstruct a given historical event. **(e)** make simple comparisons between pieces of evidence and to list the important aspects of two or more without necessarily drawing conclusions from them. **(f)** communicate in an understandable form.	**(e)** demonstrate the limitations of a particular piece of evidence; identify deficiencies in sources and to indicate other types of evidence that the historian would need to refer to in relation to the topic or event in question. **(f)** contrast and compare two or more different sorts of evidence, and demonstrate where they either support or contradict each other; be able to write a clear conclusion based on the evidence provided. **(g)** communicate clearly, coherently and accurately.
	Grade A	
	In order to be awarded **Grade A**, a candidate will be expected to achieve all the expectations of a Grade C but with subtle and important differences. Far more emphasis is placed on **accuracy** and **relevance** of material. The candidate must also produce the work in a **fluent style** which shows a clear understanding of the material used. Obviously more marks are made available at this level in order to reward the candidate who can achieve all these objectives. Since every mark is important it is always essential to complete an assignment to the best of your ability.	

question, nor permit you to re-write the assignment once you have handed it in.

Some examination groups allow candidates to use material other than that in written form. If you wish to submit such material in an assignment you must discuss your ideas with your teacher before starting the exercise.

It is worth remembering that each examination group has its own individual requirements for coursework, so it is always useful to seek advice from your teacher about any aspect of it that concerns you.

Before looking in detail at specific examples of coursework assignments and how to tackle them, we shall examine carefully the chart on page 13, which shows the standards required to gain specific grades by the total GCSE course in order to give an overall picture of where coursework fits into the pattern. Again you need to remember that each group has its own grade criteria but broadly they are the same.

Remember these descriptions are shown only to give a **general** indication of the standards of achievement expected from candidates at three levels of attainment. The final grade will be awarded according to how the candidate has met the assessment objectives overall i.e. in both **coursework** and **examinations**.

In the next Section we shall look in detail at some examples of assignments and also how the levels of attainment would be allocated. Remember, though, that they are only **examples**. You should find it helpful to study the approach of students **and** teachers, even though you may not be studying the same topics or periods.

✓ **Checklist**

1 For the final grade you will normally be permitted to submit the best assignments from each category from those you have attempted throughout the two year course.

2 Usually your assignments will be marked in your own school.

3 The teacher will construct a mark scheme which will reward **positive** responses to the assignment.

4 The prime aim of any assignment is the fulfilment of the objective.

5 It is worth seeking advice from your teacher before submitting work for an assignment in a non-written form.

6 It is always very important to complete an assignment to the best of your ability.

SECTION FOUR

Source-based assignments

In Section Three we looked at the criteria on which your teacher bases the marks when assessing assignments. These have to conform to a pattern laid down by the examination group. This mark is added to the mark you attain in the final examination and then a final grade is awarded by the group. In this Section we examine examples of coursework assignments and show how the marks would be allocated to different answers based on the **levels of response** shown in Section Three.

Remember that in most assignments you will be expected to answer questions using a variety of **different sources**. These will depend on the subject matter you have studied but they are unlikely to be types you have not experienced before.

Assignment 1

The following example is a GCSE coursework assignment based on source material dealing with the Second World War. The **assessment objective** tests 'the understanding and interpretation of historical evidence'. It is divided into two parts. Part 1, containing seven sources of information, deals with the evacuation of Dunkirk. Part 2 contains eight sources dealing with the German invasion of the USSR. Each part carries 25 marks. As in all assignments and exam work be sure to read the **instructions**, the **sources** and the **questions** very carefully.

Part 1: The evacuation of Dunkirk

Study the following sources carefully and answer the questions about them.

Source A: Figure 4.1 shows the painting of the evacuation of Dunkirk, by Charles Cundall.

Fig. 4.1 The evacuation of Dunkirk

Source B: Winston Churchill remembers the plan to evacuate soldiers from Dunkirk.

> Everyone who had a boat of any kind, steam or sail set out for Dunkirk . . . Nearly 400 small craft played a vital part in ferrying from the beaches to the off-lying ships nearly 1000 men.

Source C: Winston Churchill speaking to the House of Commons about Dunkirk, 5 June 1940.

> A miracle was achieved by valour, perseverance, perfect discipline and skill. The enemy was hurled back by the retreating French and British troops and so roughly handled that he did not disturb the departure plans seriously. The Royal Air Force engaged the German airfire and inflicted on them losses of four to one. The Navy rescued 335 000 men, both French and British.

Source D: Figure 4.2 shows a photograph of the scene at Dunkirk, 1940.

Fig. 4.2 The scene at Dunkirk

Source E: A German fighter pilot remembers Dunkirk.

> I hated Dunkirk. It was just cold-blooded killing. The beaches were jammed with soldiers. I went up and down spraying them with bullets.

Source F: A British pilot remembers Dunkirk. An RAF pilot, shot down near Dunkirk, tells of what he saw when he reached the beaches.

> Most of the men were exhausted. Snake-like lines of men stretched from the sand-dunes to the water's edge. When there was an air attack everyone ran for cover. Mostly, the troops just dived into the the water, up to their necks. They would then fire their rifles at the planes. The bombs fell, machine gun-fire swept the beaches. In a few seconds the raids were over. A number of British soldiers would not be needing transport to England.

Source G: An historian, C. Bayne-Jardine, sums up the results of the Dunkirk evacuation.

> The weather remained fine and on 3 June 1940 the last of the 338 226 men taken off from Dunkirk clambered on board a rescue ship. Almost the entire BEF and nearly 140 000 French troops had been saved, though all the army's heavy equipment, six destroyers and 474 aeroplanes had been lost in the process.

Questions

1 (a) Explain the part played by small boats at Dunkirk. *(4)*

(b) Explain the part played by the RAF at Dunkirk. *(4)*

2 Compare the account of the evacuation in source **C** with the accounts in sources **E** and **F**. How can you explain the differences between them? *(8)*

3 'The evacuation at Dunkirk was a miracle.' After studying the evidence, do you agree that the rescue of over 300 000 men *was* miraculous? *(8)*

4 Are photographs as in source **D** more reliable as historical evidence than paintings as in source **A**? *(8)*

5 Using the sources *and* your own knowledge explain the results and consequences of the Dunkirk operation. *(8)*

6 Write about the reliability and usefulness of the written sources in helping historians to reach conclusions about what happened at Dunkirk.

(a) Which of the sources are more reliable?

(b) Which of the sources are less reliable?

(c) What are the limitations of the sources? *(10)*

At this stage the student would go on to Part 2. However, to simplify matters we will examine the **mark scheme** for this section of the assessment and see how two candidates were awarded marks. (**L1** means Level 1, etc.)

Mark scheme

The evacuation of Dunkirk 1940

1(a) *(4)* **1(b)** *(4)* **2** *(8)* **3** *(8)* **4** *(8)* **5** *(8)* **6** *(10)*   **Total:** *(50)*

Question 1

(a) **L1** states part played
- lifts information from source *(1)*
- paraphrases some *(2)*   *(1-2)*

L2 explains part played
- weak explanation *(3)*
- developed/clear *(4)*   *(3-4)*

e.g. ferrying men from beaches, L1, *(1)*
going backwards and forwards with soldiers taking them to the ships, L1, *(2)*
because the big ships couldn't get close to shore, L2, *(3)*
as they would go around in the shallow water, *(4)*

(b) Exactly as question **1(a)**
e.g. RAF engaged the enemy, L1, *(1)*
RAF fought the German planes and defeated them usually, L1, *(2)*
this protected the allied soldiers, L2, *(3)*
since they couldn't shoot them or bomb them while they were fighting the RAF, L2, *(4)*   *(1-4)*

Question 2

L1 Writes the differences–virtually no attempt to discuss them *(1-2)*

L2 Writes some differences, some attempt to explain them with (occasional) references to sources *(3-5)*

L3 Fuller account of a range of differences–explains, perhaps with reference to motives of writers of the sources *(6-8)*

Question 3

L1 Agrees or disagrees with the statement in the question, simple supporting statement, scant reference to the evidence provided *(1-2)*

L2 Agrees, showing some comprehension of the sources, **OR** disagrees, uses information from sources to support view e.g. in the light of source **E**, it was amazing that they were not all killed *(3-4)*

L3 Balanced answer; sees evidence provided is conflicting:
- in some ways it could be considered a miracle, in some ways not
- depends on how you look at it *(5-6)*

L4 Sees limitations of sources (e.g. Churchill's was propaganda) and incompleteness of sources:
- How many men were there at Dunkirk?
- What percentage of soldiers were killed, captured, rescued? *(7-8)*

NB Answers which concentrate on incompleteness of sources without using the evidence provided, maximum of L2.

Question 4

L1 Yes/no statements with simple non-historical reason to support them, e.g. photo of actual event is more reliable than painting which is imagination or artistic skill *(1-2)*

L2 Yes/no statement concentrating on one source showing it to be reliable/unreliable *(3-5)*

L3 Answers could conclude either way (yes/no) but answer brings out weak/strong points of both sources; top mark reserved for relevant conclusion based on historical argument *(6-8)*

Question 5

L1 Lists some results, makes little comment, offers virtually no explanation or reference to source *(1-2)*

L2 Lists some results, offers some comment(s) by way of development or explanation; clear but limited reference to one or two of the sources could be made *(3-4)*

L3 Able to discriminate at a deeper level among the consequences (immediate/longterm results; more important results; trifling matters); refers to several sources; introduces some 'own knowledge' relevantly *(5-6)*

L4 Good, clear understanding of various relevant issues, i.e. able to infer relationships of consequences; uses own knowledge e.g. 'loss of material not too bad: get it back from USA' **OR**
'they were able to continue the war' and 'later be in a position to win it' *(7-8)*

Question 6

L1 Vague assertions/statements about what the evidence says without reference to the nature of the evidence *(1-2)*

L2 Shows some ability to handle evidence without addressing the question set; e.g. primary is reliable, secondary is unreliable **OR** all sources are useful, without specific reference to sources on Dunkirk *(3-5)*

L3 Deals superficially with reliability or usefulness **OR** deals thoroughly with one but not the other e.g. Churchill's evidence (source **C**) biased, propaganda, etc., so unreliable, but useful—we see what Churchill wanted people to believe *(6-8*

L4 Balanced treatment of reliability and utility with references to specific sources as examples; sees advantages/disadvantages with all of the sources *(9-10)*

NB Both the following examples have been printed as they were written by the candidates. The punctuation and spelling are as they were in their scripts.

Fig. 4.3 Candidate A's answer

The Evacuation of Dunkirk

1.a.   The small boats played a very important part in Dunkirk. Nearly 400 small boats (whether they were steam powered, or sail/wind powered) went to Dunkirk, and rescued nearly 1000 men from the beaches. The Royal Navy needed help to get right up to the shore.

b.   The R.A.F. also played a very important in the rescue, they defended the British troops, which were being gunned down by the German planes. So the RAF were trying to shoot down the German airforce so to defend the rescue boats + ships, and the soldiers.

2.   In scource 'C', Winston Churchill is praising the success of Dunkirk, and also he is speaking to the House of Commons. So he doesn't want to look stupid infront of them.
      In Sources 'E' and 'F', they are accounts from people who actually took part in the war. They are from the two opposite sides, but they still tell the same thing : – the horror of Dunkirk. Sources 'E' + 'F' are primary evidence, where as source 'C' is secondary evidence.

3.   The evacuation of Dunkirk was described as a miracle, but I wouldn't go as far as to say that. A miracle is something like what Jesus performed. Dunkirk was planned, but still many died, lots of equipment that was essential to the British was destroyed or left behind, planes + boats were bombed. So Dunkirk wasn't really a miracle so to **speak**. It really depends how you look at it, it was very clever how they saved many men, but yet many soldiers from both sides, Germans, French + British, lost their lives.

Continued

Fig. 4.3 Continued

4. Photographs are much more reliable as evidence than paintings. This is because, a photograph is an actual correct portrayl of an event, but it could be a one-sided view. But therefore, a painting is a portrayl of what the artist wants you to see. A painting is a bias point of view.

5. The Dunkirk operation was a sucess, it rescued over 335 000 men, these included French and British forces. But some people may see the rescue as a failure, the men that actually took part may have said it was unorginised and caused too many deaths. The beaches were just a ~~blood~~ cold-blooded killing ground.

   Many British citizens who were owners of a boat of any kind, all pulled together as one, to help rescue the British and French troops.

6. Source A is fairly reliable, but it is a painting, which only shows the view of the artist. We are seeing what the artist wants us to see, a bias point of view. Source B is a reliable source of evidence, as it is recounting what Winston Churchill said, it is just stating the motive of Dunkirk's rescue. Source C isn't very reliable, its Winston Churchill telling the house of commons about Dunkirk, he is praising it, + telling them it was a success. He wouldn't really tell them it was a failure as they would say that Churchill couldn't do his job properly. Source D is a photograph, which shows the truth but again is a biased point of view. Source E + F are reliable, as they are accounts ~~of~~ by men who took part in Dunkirk - primary evidence. Source G is secondary evidence + reliable to a point. Sources E + F are the most reliable, and Source A is the less reliable. You can only get so much information from these sources.

Fig. 4.4 Candidate B's answer

1a. The small boats at Dunkirk sail from home parts in england and ferried soilders from the beach to the larger ships further out. This was so the big ships didn't have to go so far in and risk getting beached or sunk.

b. The RAF also played an important part at Dunkirk they helped to keep the German pilots out of the sky's so they couldn't bomb the beaches or the small boats and large ships. Without the RAF many more men would have been lost and many more ships would have been lost. The RAF managed to stop the bombers bombing by engaging them in battle although a few got through those fighting could not drop their bombs because they couldn't get to the beaches.

2. In source C Winston Churchill is praising the mission of Dunkirk. Being leader of the war effort in Britain he is forced into such a statement whether it is true or not. This speech is biased in that it only mentions Britain's successes. It is propaganda to give the British people hope. Sources E and F show a more realistic account. Both tell us that many British troops were killed disproving Churchill's statement that the German's did not disturb the departure plans seriously.'
Source C describes a perfect mission with only minor air and land losses. It is a miracle of skill and valour.
In Source E the German pilot describes how he shot many soldiers although this too may be biased. In Source F the English pilot tells us of exhausted troops and repeated German air attacks. I think that sources E and F have less reason to be biased than Source c.

3. I do not think that the evacuation was a miracle.

Continued

Fig. 4.4 *Continued*

The events described by Winston Churchill were dubious as to their reality. In his speech he was probably trying to boost morale of his troops and was able to exagerate the success of the mission. The Dunkirk mission was a success as it did save 340 000 men but it was hardly a success of miraculous proportions. Many troops were lost and all the heavy machinery was abandoned. Also boats and aircraft were destroyed. The rescue was a well planned and well carried out operation but was not a miracle.

4. Photographs are more reliable than paintings, because a photograph captures a still frame of what was happening at one time, its weakness is that it was only one moment in time but it can not really be questioned as being a fake as it is unlikely that anyone would doctor a photo like that. The painting has something of a mystery about it as the text in source A does not show us who painted this and on what date so the painting could have been painted by somebody who wasn't there and just painted it afterwards on people's experiences or if the people's experiences were dull he may have just painted it on his imagination. So both photograph and picture are unreliable as evidence for the reasons I put.

5. The main result of Dunkirk was that Britain ~~got~~ got 300 000 men safely back to G.B. although six destroyers and 474 aeroplanes and all the army's heavy equipment was lost britain could continue fighting because they had the men to put into battle and the equipment could be rebuilt. The main consequence was as I have

Continued

Fig. 4.4 *Continued*

mentioned that britain could fight and this proved to be fatal for Germany as they eventually lost the war.

6. The sources which I believe to be the most reliable are the accounts and descriptions said by people directly involved there and then for example the British pilot and German because they had primary information which is most useful to the historian. Sources which I think are less reliable are ones which were not <u>actually</u> at the scene eg Source G is a summing up and is secondary information another scource which I believe to be less reliable is Source A the painting because it was done after and also source C by Winston Churchill because they were not at the scene and therefore we cannot say that they are totally true. The limitations of the sources are that they only captured at one point of the war and at one place at one time and the sources are also byast towards the country of their origin so you can't totally believe the sources to contain the true facts.

Note that the first candidate did not display the level of understanding necessary to gain the high level response and therefore the higher marks.

Part 2: The German invasion of the USSR

Study the following sources carefully and answer the questions about them.

Source H: Figure 4.5 shows a map showing the German invasion of Russia in 1941.

Source I: Hitler's view of the state of Russia in 1941.

> We have only to kick in the door and the whole rotten structure will come crashing down.

Source J: A German soldier describes the conditions in which he was living during the winter of 1941.

> Day after day, night after night, we sit in the open air, and a rain of artillery and small arms fire pours over us. We think our feet will freeze at any moment. And we've no real billets. We are standing, 30 of us, in a room 3 metres by 5 metres. No windows. Nor can we heat the place, lest the smoke discloses our whereabouts. But our men, they go on standing. They can't be beaten. It is an act of heroism even greater than that of the World War. It is the most fabulous epoch of German soldiery.

Fig. 4.5 The German invasion of Russia in 1941

Source K: The Battle of Stalingrad: Hitler's attitude to the German armies. In November, Russian armies broke through north and south of Stalingrad. The Germans in Stalingrad found that they were surrounded. Paulus asked Hitler several times for permission to break out of the city. Each time Hitler said, 'no'. At the end of November, Paulus radioed to Hitler.

> My Fuhrer, ammunition and fuel are nearly used up. The army is about to be completely destroyed. We must break out now. Many of our guns will be left behind but most of our men can be saved.

Hitler's answer was:

> Stalingrad must be held at all costs.

Source L: General Zeitzler describes the feelings of the average German soldier fighting at Stalingrad during the winter of 1942.

> For the ordinary soldier fighting at Stalingrad each day simply brought a renewed dose of hunger, need, privation, hardship of every sort, bitter cold, loneliness of soul, hopelessness . . .

Source M: The results of the Battle of Stalingrad from a history textbook.

> By the end of January, 1943, the famous sixth army which swept through Holland and Belgium in 1940 was worn out in Stalingrad. Paulus and his staff surrendered in a basement to a Russian lieutenant and the remains of the sixth army were taken prisoner. The Russians suffered terrible losses in this battle; they lost more men in Stalingrad than the Americans lost on all fronts in the war. Yet the defeat of the sixth army proved that the Germans could be defeated.

Source N: Figure 4.6 shows the cartoonist Low's view of the importance of the Russian defence of their country.

IN THE PAGES OF HISTORY

Fig. 4.6 A cartoon by Low

Source O: How the war in Russia affected other war fronts (from a history textbook).

> On 11 December, Auckinleck attacked and Rommel, whose reserves had been weakened to send help to the Russian Front, fell back.

Questions

1 Look at source **H**. Explain Hitler's plan for attacking Russia in 1941. *(5)*

2 Using the sources and your own knowledge, explain why the German attack ground to a halt in December 1941. *(5)*

3 (a) Is the cartoonist Low sympathetic to the Germans or to the Russians? Explain your answer. *(4)*
(b) How useful are cartoons to historians studying historical topics such as the Second World War? *(6)*

4 Sources **J, K, L** and **M** all give information about conditions and atmosphere among the Germans and Stalingrad. How can you explain the differences between source **J** and the other three sources? *(8)*

5 (a) Choose one example of a **primary source** and one example of a **secondary source**. Write fully the reasons for your choice in each case. *(4)*
(b) Which of the two sources you have chosen is the more reliable? Give reasons for your answer. *(6)*

6 What can you learn from these sources about Hitler's strengths and weaknesses as a military leader? *(12)*

Mark scheme

The German Invasion of the USSR

1 *(5)* **2** *(5)* **3** *(10)* **4** *(8)* **5** *(10)* **6** *(12)*   **Total**: *(50)*

Question 1

L1 Answers make one or two valid points, but do not explain plan as a whole *(1-2)*

L2 Answers use the map to provide a full explanation of Hitler's plan of attack; top mark for explicit use of map *(3-5)*

Question 2

L1 Answers make one or two valid points, but information is limited to simple statement or is drawn from only one source *(1-2)*

L2 Answers make fuller use of sources and own knowledge, e.g. source **G** (map) vast areas conquered; long supply lines source **J**: exposure to freezing cold of winter. Own knowledge: large numbers of POWs taken Russian tactics on retreat; top mark for direct use of sources *(3-5)*

Question 3

(a) L1 Simple obvious reference to cartoon *(1)*
Lowe is British: favours Russia *(1)* } both *(2)* *(1-2)*
L2 Explains reference to cartoon *(3)*
Explains why GB would sympathize with Russia *(3)* } both *(4)* *(3-4)*
(b) L1 Useful because it gives us information –vague, *(1)*
gives simple example *(1)* *(1-2)*

L2 Useful because it tells us what people (vague) thought at the time–information about attitudes etc. useful–adds to our knowledge of the event (must show how) *(3-4)*

L3 Limited use because view of cartoonist only–may be general view; limited because cartoonist biased so that he produces picture/joke that would appeal to an audience–shows what cartoonist thinks people would welcome–not necessarily truth *(5-6)*

Question 4

L1 Descriptive only–just describes differences: no attempt to explain them *(1-2)*

L2 Full account of differences–explains only one difference fully: or vague or irrelevant, explains generally *(3-4)*

L3 Explains differences in that they are written by different people at different times, so obviously would be different; source **J** a soldier; source **K** General Paulus; source **L** another general, source **H** a textbook much later; good attempt to tackle question *(5-6)*

L4 Brings out the significance of extra years of fighting—prolonged/ repeated misery: appalling nature of the fighting and shortages; effect on morale of *2nd* winter;
source **K** 'on the point of destruction'
source **M** 'loneliness of soul, hopelessness'
source **N** 'worn out' *(7-8)*

Question 5

5 (a) Primary sources **I, J, L, N**
Secondary sources **H, M, O**
K is both, secondary but includes primary (radio message)

L1 Correct identification *(1-2)*
Primary: from actual time by persons involved, living then
Secondary: written later by someone not there using other people's reports of evidence

L2 Justifies choice: *(3-4)*

(b) L1 Primary reliable; secondary is unreliable *(1)*
Primary is more reliable because it came first *(2)* *(1-2)*

L2 **Primary** is more reliable because the person was there—should have known what is what like: **OR**
secondary, person not there and wouldn't know *(3-4)*
secondary is more reliable because writer has time to check more sources/other people's work/dust has settled etc.
Primary—knowledge limited to that incident/time only

L3 Both equally could be reliable or unreliable; balanced answer shows advantages and limitations of **both** sources: both equally open to **bias** etc. *(5-6)*

Question 6

L1 Bold statements based on only partly understood or limited evidence: Hitler was good general—wanted Stalingrad held at all costs **OR** Hitler was bad general—he let lots of men suffer and die *(1-2)*

L2 Valid argument given but limited because it is based on only one or two pieces of evidence—does not see that Hitler was good in some ways and bad in others *(3-4)*

L3 Balanced answer sees both positive and negative qualities in Hitler's leadership, but makes only one or two points based on flimsy evidence *(5-7)*

L4 Balanced answer based on full range of sources to back up points made (which may of course appear in L3) *(8-10)*

L5 Balanced answer which realizes that some sources contain evidence for both views within them e.g. source **J**—bad general lets men fight in bad conditions but good general gets men to fight heroically for him **AND/OR**
source **K**—bad general should have spared the men's lives but good general still obeyed by men even though they were at extremes of desparation and he was thousands of miles away *(11-12)*

*** L5 also, if a balanced, detailed account is given (L4) and the candidate says, 'We do not have enough sources to make a valid judgment . . .'
If candidate gives vague answer and says, 'We can't tell—not enough evidence,' place top L2 or bottom L3 (e.g. *4-5 marks*)

The above assignment would have been given to a class of students to be completed within a defined period of time, usually a number of history lessons. This example was actually completed in a double period lasting 80 minutes.

It could also be used as a **controlled assignment**, completed under examination conditions. As you can see the questions become more difficult as they progress.

The mark scheme, allocating marks for the various levels of response, will reflect the complexity of the question. You need to remember that in general terms you will gain higher marks if you show a high level of understanding; not factual detail!

> *Higher marks will be given to answers showing high levels of understanding.*

Assignment 2   LEAG: Modern World History Assessment

The Russian Revolution

Objective: To test the ability of students to comprehend, analyse, compare and evaluate different kinds of historical evidence.

Part 1: Russia between 1900 and 1914

Study sources **A** to **E** carefully, then answer the questions about them.

Source A: Figure 4.7 shows a Russian cartoon of 1900.

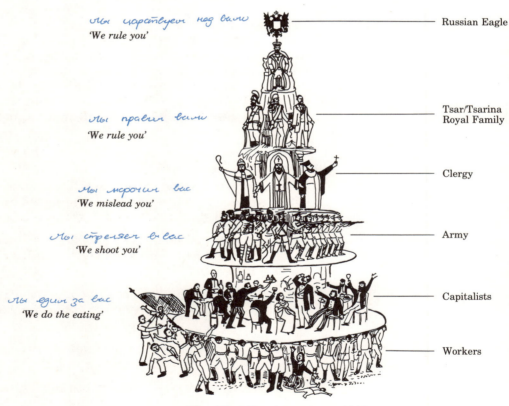

'We rule you'

'We rule you'

'We mislead you'

'We shoot you'

'We do the eating'

Russian Eagle

Tsar/Tsarina Royal Family

Clergy

Army

Capitalists

Workers

Fig. 4.7 A Russian cartoon, 1900

Source B: An extract from a book by Father Gapon, written in 1905.

They receive miserable wages and generally live in an overcrowded state, very commonly in special lodging houses. A woman takes several rooms in her own name, subletting each one; and it is common to see ten or more persons living in one room and four sleeping in one bed. The normal working day is eleven and a half hours of work, exclusive of meal times. But . . . manufacturers have received permission to work overtime, so that the average day is longer than that nominally allowed by law–fourteen or fifteen hours.

Source C: A Russian priest tells of how the peasants treated him (extract taken from the Diary of a Scottish traveller in Russia in the last years of the 19th century).

> 'I can overhear their sneers as I go away, and I know they have many sayings such as, "The priest takes from the living and from the dead." Many of them fasten their doors pretending to be away from home, and do not even take the precaution of keeping silent till I am out of hearing.'
> 'You surprise me,' I said. 'I have always heard that the Russians are a very religious people—at least, the lower classes.'
> 'So they are; but the peasantry are poor and heavily taxed. They set great importance on the sacraments, and observe the fasts, which take up nearly half of the year; but they show very little respect for their priests, who are almost as poor as themselves.'

Source D: A rich landlord's day (taken from the same diary as source **C**).

Ivan Ivanovitch's day

Ivan Ivanovitch gets up at about seven o'clock, and puts on, with the assistance of his valet-de-chambre [servant], a simple costume consisting chiefly of a faded, plentifully stained dressing gown. Having nothing in particular to do, he sits down at the open window and looks into the yard . . . Towards nine o'clock tea is announced, and he goes into the dining room . . . As this morning meal consists merely of bread and tea, it does not last long. Ivan Ivanovitch begins the work of the day by going back to his seat at the open window . . . Here he sits till the sun has so far moved round that the verandah at the back of the house is completely in the shade, when he has his arm-chair removed there, and sits till dinner time.

Dinner is the great event of the day. The food is abundant and of good quality, but mushrooms, onions and fat play a rather too important part . . . No sooner has the last dish been removed than a death-like stillness falls upon the house: It is time for the afternoon sleep.

Source E: Figure 4.8 is a Russian cartoon of 1905.

Fig. 4.8 Half a room is a working man's home – the other half behind the curtain belongs to another family

Questions

1 Look at source **A** carefully. Do you think the cartoonist is a friend of the Tsar or supporter of the workers? Explain your answer. *(5)*

2 What is the cartoonist in source **A** trying to tell us about Russian society in 1900? Do sources **B** to **E** suggest to you that his view is correct? Explain your answer with reference to as many of sources **B** to **F** as you can. *(10)*

Part 2: The March Revolution of 1917

Study sources **F** to **J** carefully, then answer the questions about them.

Source F: A letter from the Tsarina to the Tsar.

> The whole trouble comes from these idlers, well-dressed people, wounded soldiers, highschool girls etc. . . . Lily* spoke to some cab-drivers to find out about things. They told her that the students came to them and told them that if they appeared in the streets in the morning, they would be shot to death. What corrupt minds! Of course the cab-drivers and the motormen are now on strike. But they say it is all different from 1905 because they all worship you and only want bread.

> *Lily was a lady in waiting to the Tsarina

Source G: From the diary of Sybil Grey, an Englishwoman in Petrograd in 1917.

> On Thursday 8 March a poor woman entered a bread shop on the Morskaia* and asked for bread. She was told there was none. On leaving the shop, seeing bread in the window, she broke the window and took it. A general, passing in his motor, stopped and remonstrated with her.** A crowd collected around them, smashed his motor car, and increasing in size, paraded the streets asking for bread.

> *a shopping street in Petrograd
> **told her off

Source H: A telegram from the President of the Duma to the Tsar.

> The situation is serious. The capital is in a state of anarchy. The government is paralyzed; the transport service is broken down; the food and fuel supplies are completely disorganized. Discontent is general and on the increase. There is wild shooting on the streets; troops are firing at each other. It is urgent that someone enjoying the confidence of the country be entrusted with the formation of a new government.

Source I: From the diary of a French diplomat living in Petrograd in 1917.

> The movement has taken on a political character . . . In the square in front of the Kazan Cathedral there are reserves of infantry . . . The troops opened fire in the Nevsky Prospekt* at about six o'clock . . . Most of the rounds were blank . . . All the same there were some killed and wounded.'

> *Petrograd's main street

Source J: A telegram from the Tsar to the Commander of forces in Petrograd.

> I command you to put an end as from tomorrow to all disturbances in the streets.

Questions

3 Study sources **F** and **H**. Compare the two views expressed about the troubles in Petrograd in 1917 and explain why the accounts are so different. *(8)*

4 Read the Tsar's order to his Commander in Chief (source **J**). Do you think he thought the trouble in Petrograd was very serious? *(5)*

5 Do you think the Tsar and Tsarina really knew what was going on in Petrograd in March 1917? Use sources **F, G, H, I** and **J** to help you explain your answer. *(10)*

Part 3: The November Revolution of 1917

Study the following sources **K** to **O** carefully, then answer the questions about them.

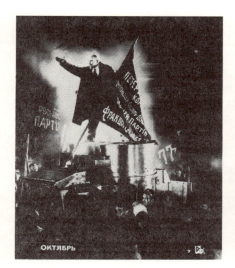

Fig. 4.9 Still shots from '10 days that shook the world'

Source K: Figure 4.9 shows two still shots from a film by the Russian director, Sergei Eisenstein in 1927: '10 days that shook the world'.

Source L: An extract from the diary of Meriel Buchanan, the daughter of the British Ambassador in Petrograd.

> At six in the evening a message was sent in to them calling on them to surrender immediately, but as no answer was received the attack on the Palace was opened by a few blank rounds being fired from the fortress as a prelimary warning. This was followed by a massed onslaught from all sides, armoured cars and machine guns firing at the palace from under the archway on the square, while now and then the guns of the fortress or of the cruiser *Aurora* thundered and crashed above the general din. Actually, however, a good many of the shots were only gun-cotton, and the firing in all cases was so inaccurate that the palace was only hit three times from the river.

Source M: An extract from the memoirs of Alexander Kerensky about the events of the November Revolution.

> **'The Cossacks fail to help**:
>
> The hours of the night dragged on painfully. From everywhere we expected reinforcements, but none appeared. There were endless telephone negotiations with the Cossack regiments. Under various excuses the Cossacks stubbornly stuck to their barracks, asserting all the time that 'everything would be cleared up' within fifteen or twenty minutes and that they would then 'begin to saddle their horses'
> . . . Meanwhile the night hours passed . . . Not a word from the Cossacks . . .'

Source N: Figure 4.10 shows two photographs of Red Guardsmen.

Fig. 4.10
Red
Guardsmen

Source O: From a history textbook by Josh Brooman.

> The provisional government had its headquarters in the Winter Palace and was guarded only by army cadets and the Women's Battalion of the army. In the evening of 7 November a cruiser, the *Aurora*, which Bolshevik sailors had captured, sailed up the River Neva and fired blank shells at the Winter Palace. Later the guns in the Peter and Paul fortress also opened fire on the Palace. Then the Red Guards stormed the Winter Palace. The cadets and the Women's Battalion gave in without a fight. The ministers of the provisional government surrendered and were taken away under arrest.

> The Bolsheviks now controlled Petrograd, the capital of Russia. The next day Lenin announced that he was setting up a new government. The Bolsheviks had come to power after a single day of rebellion in which eighteen people had been arrested and two people had been killed.

Questions

6 Read source **L**.

(a) List two different types of weapons used by the Bolsheviks in the storming of the Winter Palace.

(b) Why were the attacks on the Winter Palace during the Bolshevik Revolution so ineffective? *(4)*

7 Source **K** is taken from a film made in 1927. It is therefore a secondary source. Does this mean it is reliable or unreliable? *(8)*

8 Judging from the information contained in sources **L, M, N** or **O**, how historically accurate do you think Eisenstein's film of the storming of the Winter Palace was? Explain your answer. *(10)*

Provisional marking scheme
The Russian Revolution LEAG 1988

1 *(5)* **2** *(10)* **3** *(8)* **4** *(5)* **5** *(10)* **6** *(4)* **7** *(8)* **8** *(10)*   **Total**: *(60)*

Part 1–Russia in 1900

Question 1

L1 Something gained from cartoon but message misunderstood e.g. friend of Tsar because the Tsar is at the top of the column *(1-2)*

L2 Appreciates that cartoonist is sympathetic to the workers; gives rational explanation for his cartoon *(3-5)*

Question 2

L1 One or two random statements made about the cartoon and sources but sections merely quoted; no attempt at interpretation *(1-2)*

L2 Simple interpretation of sources; basic message of cartoon understood; cross-references made with one or two other sources (probably sources **B** and **E**) *(3-5)*

L3 Complex interpretation of sources; cartoon understood and all the sources **B** to **E** used to back up cartoon's statement *(6-8)*

L4 As with level 3, but questions raised as to whether historical judgments can be made from so narrow a range of sources. Could source **E** be typical of usual living conditions? Were all landlords like Ivan Ivanovitch, etc? Alternatively, knowledge of historical context given, in answer which shows appreciation of basic reliability of sources *(9-10)*

Part 2–The March Revolution

Question 3

L1 Comparison of sources made but no explanation of differences *(1-2)*

L2 Simple explanation made as to differences–'President of Duma was an eye-witness; Tsarina depended on secondhand evidence, etc' *(3-5)*

L3 Purposes of authors of both sources examined: Tsarina concerned to boost husband's morale minimizes difficulties; President of Duma wants Tsar to resign, stresses changes *(6-8)*

Question 4

L1 Tsar thought situation serious, asked for help from army *(1-2)*

L2 Interprets mood of Tsar's telegrams; Tsar thinks matter can be resolved quickly with little effort, so orders sound complacent *(3-5)*

Question 5

L1 Answer picks out one or two statements lifted straight from text without explanation to answer question *(1-2)*

L2 Simple explanations of answer shows how Tsarina's letter to the Tsar does not give same impression as any of the other sources *(3-5)*

L3 Looks at all sources in turn and compares their likely reliability with the Tsarina's statement; attempts to show how the Tsar could keep in touch with the situation in Petrograd *(6-8)*

L4 As with level 3 but some attempt to look beyond sources to historical context surrounding them; the Tsarina's letter interpreted in context of her notorious lack of knowledge of the details of Petrograd life; eye-witness accounts placed in historical context, etc *(9-10)*

Part 3–The November Revolution

Question 6

L1 Two weapons correctly listed from source L and makes simple statements 'lifted' from source to answer question *(1-2)*

L2 Explains clearly why various methods of attack were ineffective e.g. inaccurate shooting/shots of guncotton *(3-4)*

Question 7

L1 Misunderstands question, sees film at face value only (no shots of fighting so not reliable) *(1-2)*

L2 Problem of film partially but not totally explained; film secondary source so not particularly reliable–not as reliable as primary sources *(3-5)*

L3 Different purposes of film makers appreciated; depends on what film maker had in mind when producing film *(6-8)*

Question 8

L1 No cross-referencing or interpretation; may quote passage from one or two sources but no explanation of relevance *(1-2)*

L2 Sees some conflict between film image of storming of Winter Palace and historical records of the period; believes Eisenstein 'biased', cannot say why *(3-5)*

L3 Appreciates film as vehicle for propaganda in a state as well as documentary evidence; realizes obvious conflicts with other sources even though some of these may have their own bias *(6-8)*

L4 As with level 3 but able to grasp more clearly than L3 historical context under which Eisenstein filmed; also, some questioning of the remaining sources–can they be taken at face value? What would Meriel Buchanan's bias be, etc? *(9-10)*

Answering the question

Using the question to identify the type of answer required

In some questions in both your coursework and your final exam you will find clues to how you should answer the question. Basically, any question will ask you to do one of two things: either **describe** something in the source material or an event related to it, or **assess** and make a judgment on specific details or knowledge. The clues as to whether it is a

descriptive or an **assessment** answer or a combination of both can be found in the title. In the case of coursework it will be set and assessed by your class teacher who should indicate what is expected of your answer.

To help you we have listed below a few examples of the key phrases which provide the clues. It is of course impossible to provide details about all the types of questions you are likely to come across in your study.

Describe

Example

'Using the source material available describe the life of a factory worker before the Ten Hours Act.'

Obviously this question is asking for a general description of the worker's life and nothing else. It does not require you to make any judgments, but you must use the source material as it asks.

How?

Example

'How did the life of a factory worker improve after 1847?'

Again the answer to this needs only a description of the improvements that were made, but in order to answer this effectively and gain the highest levels you would need to include a description of the life of the factory worker before, and after, the date given in the question.

What?

Be very careful with any question starting with the word 'what', as either a descriptive or an analytical answer can be required. These questions need to be read with extreme care.

Example

'What changes were brought about by the introduction of the Ten Hour Act?'

This requires a descriptive answer 'listing' all the changes that took place.

Example

'What did the Ten Hour Act achieve?'

This requires your assessment and judgment of the achievement, or otherwise, of the Act and again needs some knowledge of the working conditions before its introduction.

If you are given pictorial sources and asked, 'What are the names given to the machines labelled A and B in source **C**?' you only need to give the names, nothing else.

Discuss

Any question starting with the word 'discuss' needs you to analyse the facts and details in a particular topic or course.

Example

'Discuss the significance of the Ten Hour Act on industrial practices in the 19th century.'

This requires an analysis of the impact of the Act. It does not ask for a description of the Act itself.

Why?

Example

'Why was the open field system admirably suited to earlier times?'

The word 'why' suggests that you analyse the reasons why the system was suited to earlier times. It is not enough just to describe the system, you must go on to show the ways in which it was suited to the time.

> *Questions beginning with 'what' should be read very carefully.*

Explain

Example

'Explain why Krushchev fell from power in 1964.'

This requires a statement of the position of Krushchev in 1964 and an analysis of the events which led to his eventual removal from power later in the year.

At the beginning of your GCSE course it would be worth asking your teacher to explain the wording of any question you do not understand. Reading the question properly is a very important skill which has to be learned like any other.

Checklist

1 Remember, in most assignments you will be expected to answer questions from a variety of sources.

2 These sources are unlikely to be examples you have not experienced before.

3 In all assignments and exam work make sure you read the instructions, source material and questions **very carefully**.

4 Assignments can be given as part of your normal history lessons in class or as a **controlled assignment** completed under exam conditions.

5 Often the questions become more difficult as they progress.

6 The more understanding of the topic you display in your answer the higher the **level of response** marks you will gain.

7 Supplementary detail in your answers from the work you have done in class **must** be relevant.

8 Clues as to how a question needs to be answered can often be found in the question itself. Generally speaking questions starting with, or including, the words 'describe', 'how', 'give an account of', and some beginning with 'what' require descriptive answers. Those questions starting with, or including, the words 'explain', 'discuss', 'why' and some beginning with 'what' require assessment or analytical answers. Remember there are exceptions to this rule so each question should be read very carefully.

9 Be very careful when answering any question beginning with 'what'!

Empathy

The skill of **empathy** or the ability to **empathize** with a character, or group of characters, is important in the study of history. It has become an integral part of the GCSE syllabus.

An empathetic exercise does not simply require you to put yourself in the place of an historical character or group of people. It is one which demands great skill and all round knowledge. The exercise you will be given by your teacher will be designed to give you the opportunity to display an awareness of the ways in which other people and societies differ from your own. You should also show how political, religious and economic factors have helped to produce these differences. You will be expected to describe an historical situation as it appeared **at the time** to the people who actually **experienced** it. You will be tested on your ability to understand **other people's** points of view, their problems and difficulties, their emotions and feelings, and be able to anticipate their reactions to specific situations. It is a part of the syllabus which requires a certain amount of sensitivity especially in exercises needing understanding of people and events in totally different cultures from your own.

When dealing with controversial political issues such as the Middle East, Northern Ireland or British Parliamentary politics (e.g. Labour v Conservative), a **balanced** stance must be portrayed, with due attention being paid to a **range** of views, rather than partisan ideas. When writing an answer dealing with these matters it must be remembered that equally strong views can be held on **both** sides and that **not all** people hold these strong views; some hold moderate views and some have no strong political view at all. They just wish violence and arguments would stop. The examination group is **not** seeking a judgment on who is right.

> *An empathy answer must be based on clear historical evidence. It is not a piece of imaginative writing!*

The most important object of such an exercise is that you, as the candidate, must base your answer on clear, real, **historical evidence** and **knowledge**. It is not expected to be a piece of imaginary writing such as you might write in an English lesson.

Most examination groups will allow the candidate to write the answer either in the first person: 'I did . . . .' or in the third person: 'He/they did . . .' However you decide to write it, you will be required to use and display a number of historical skills:
- the ability to understand the practices and actions of people in other societies
- the ability to reconstruct the attitudes and beliefs of those people or individuals
- the ability to interpret motivation in history.

Remember you will not be writing this assignment as though you are putting **yourself back** in time. You must imagine how **the character** felt **then**, not how **you** would have felt had **you** been there yourself. You are asked to provide a description of an event **not** as an observer but **more** as a participant.

To gain high marks in an empathy exercise you need to have a good understanding and knowledge of the period of history the question relates to. Your answer will therefore need to **reflect** this knowledge and be **based on fact**.

Mark schemes

The marks for each of the questions on empathy would be allocated according to a standard format common to all examining groups.

Level 1 Everyday empathy: Where a candidate realizes that people in the past had feelings, but these feelings are limited to what present-day people could or would be likely to feel in that situation.

Level 2 Stereotyped empathy: Where a candidate is able to attribute attitudes and feelings to people in the past, and to present these in accurate historical context. Typically at this level a candidate seems to believe that all the people of the past thought in the same way.

Level 3 Differentiated empathy: Where the candidate understands attitudes as in level 2 but in addition realizes that there would be variations in what people in the past thought and felt, that is, they would react in different ways for different reasons.

There are two main ways in which an empathy assignment can be constructed.

Straight-forward accounts
Sometimes called essays

The SEG and MEG Objective 3 assignments often take this form, and a candidate needs to write 500–1000 words maximum to show understanding of the way people in the past felt. Obviously, a few different ideas could be listed in a very few sentences, but in answers to such assignments candidates must ensure that they convey a good understanding of the period and issues in question. The views cited have to be explained fully with reference to the history of the period (i.e. the 'empathy' has to be sustained and supported) if level 3 is to be attained.

Very short answers to SEG or MEG empathy assignments would not normally attract many marks.

Source-based questions

An array of sources can be used to open up the topic and focus attention on some of the issues. Here the number of questions might be greater, but the word-total of the assignment as a whole might be similar. Thus there might be four 'empathy' questions on a given theme, which could be answered in say 150–200 words each, matching the total for an essay-type assignment.

> *Correct use of sources will be rewarded.*

With these source-based questions it is important to study the sources carefully. Relevant use of the sources can receive credit. Material should not merely be copied from the sources, though. It is much better, as with assignments aimed at 'handling sources', to paraphrase the wording of the extract: you show your understanding to much better effect if you put the sense into your own words. Candidates should also be prepared to bring in and add information drawn from their fund of knowledge where this is required and relevant.

The two assignments in this Section could be used separately or as a whole assignment on the theme of Berlin. Some examples of candidates' responses and the method of marking follow the details of the assignments. First—a word of caution: empathy is often a controversial concept and not all history teachers are agreed on what makes a good empathy assignment or how it is best marked. These notes are offered as a guide to the latest thinking.

Examples

Imagine you have been given the following empathy exercises. There are two similar ones provided here, one on Berlin 1948 and the other on Berlin 1961. There is a total of 20 marks for each. How may the marks be allocated?

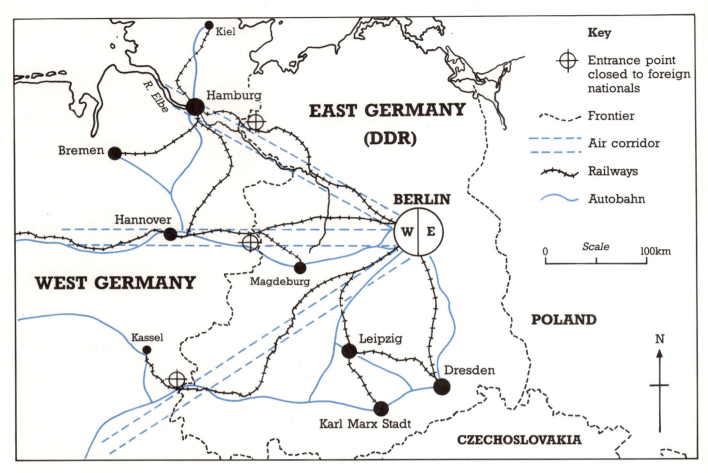

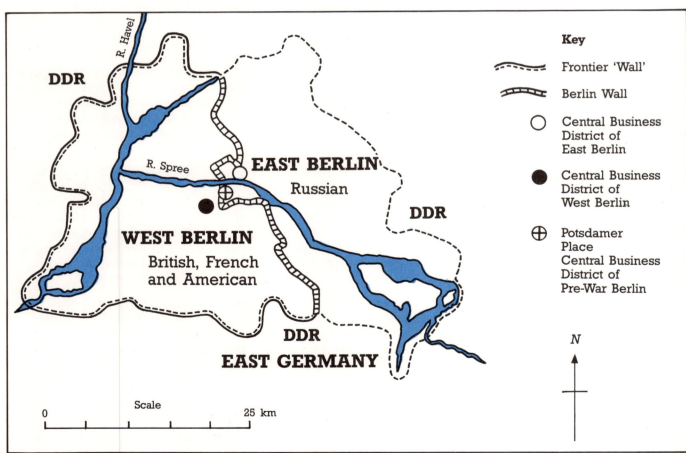

Fig. 5.1 How Germany was divided after the Second World War

Assignment 1   World Powers since 1917 (1)

Assessment testing empathy

The Berlin Question 1945–71

Study sources A to E carefully and then answer the questions about them.

Source A: Figure 5.1 shows two maps showing how Germany was divided after the Second World War.

Source B: 'The beginning of the blockade' 23 June 1948. The message from the Soviet News Agency to Berlin's main newspaper read as follows.

> The Soviet administration is compelled to halt all traffic to and from Berlin tomorrow because of technical difficulties.

Berlin was cut off from the West. Technical difficulties meant that the Russians closed all roads, canals and railways between Berlin and Western Germany. Berlin had only enough food and fuel to last six weeks.

Source C: A message from General Lucius Clay, (in charge of the American Sector in Berlin) to the commander of the US airforce in Germany, 1948.

> 'Have you any planes that can carry coal?' asked Clay.
>
> 'Carry what?' asked the startled airforce commander.
>
> 'Coal,' repeated Clay.
>
> 'We must have a bad connection,' said the airforce man. 'It sounds as if you are asking if we have planes for carrying coal.'
>
> 'Yes, that's what I said,' replied Clay.

Source D: The result of the airlift.

> Altogether some 300 000 flights were made and 2 million tons of supplies flown in.

Source E: Figure 5.2 shows a cartoon painted by a German child at the end of the airlift.

Fig. 5.2 'We thank the pilots for their work and effort.'

Questions

1 Explain the thoughts and feelings that American and British pilots might have had when they were ordered to fly supplies of coal and other materials into Berlin. *(10)*

2 How do you think the people of West Berlin would have reacted when the first planes landed, carrying vital supplies for them? *(10)*

Candidate A

I think there would have been a great variety of feelings that the American and British pilots would have had about flying supplies of coal and other materials into Berlin. To start with they might have felt that it would be a bit far too dangerous for them. and that they were sure to be shot down. Their countries had been at war and being in the airforces they had no choice about going. I think they would have been very proud that they would be saving the lives of the people of Berlin and when they discovered how easy it was to break the blockade and take food to the Berliners, they would not have minded at all, they were heroes. They were also easily breaking the communist blockade, this was a very easily won point for the bully chart of the cold war.

Fig. 5.3 Candidate A, question 1

This is a level 2 answer for the following reasons.

1 It is not enough to say that 'there could be a great variety of feelings'. To reach level 3 a candidate has to demonstrate an understanding of what those feelings were. Examples and explanations of several different views should be given.

2 The main body of the answer assumes that all pilots felt roughly the same way. The words 'they might have felt', 'they would have been proud' suggest level 2 **stereotyped empathy**.

The actual level 2 mark would not be high because, although there are some good points made which bring it into level 2, the latter part of the answer concentrates too much on how 'easy' it was for the pilots, which is inaccurate and shows lack of understanding of the context. *(L2-4)*

I think the people of Western Berlin would have been very shocked to see that the Westerners had not forgotten about them and had not left them to the mercies of the communists. I am sure many thought they were dreaming with lack of food they might start to hallucinate and would not believe what they were seeing. I think they might have been a bit hesitant to collect the supplies but as soon as they realised it was for real there would have been a mad scramble to collect food and fuel.

Fig. 5.4 Candidate A, question 2

This is a level 1 answer for the following reasons.

1 It has only one main theme or idea, which is that the people of West Berlin would all be unable to believe that the airlift was taking place. The people would all be shocked—'thought they were dreaming/hallucinating', 'hesitant to collect the supplies'.

2 The sentiments expressed are akin to what someone today might think about the situation in 1948. There is little relevant material giving context drawn from candidate's own knowledge or sources, so **everyday empathy** mark.

(L1-2)

Candidate B

Why do we feed and supply these people when, and after, they started a war in which thousands of people were killed? The other pilots in the pub tell me it's because Berlin is in East Germany. The Russian zone and as we in a sort of Cold War with them that it is of great military and economic importance because it is the capital. When we were ordered to fly the supplies in many of us could not believe it and had to check to make sure. Most of them are

Continued

Continued

quite happy as it ensures a job for the moment and they are doing what they like best - flying.

The German people are very grateful for it as well they try to give us much needed things and the children paint pictures for us.

Fig. 5.5 Candidate B, question 1

This is a level 2 answer. It gets nearer to L3 **differentiated empathy** but only suggests that a range of attitudes existed; it does not explain what other views were.
'Many of us could not believe it' = level 2 (What did others believe?)
'Most of (the pilots) were happy' = level 2 (Why were the others unhappy?)

The reference to other pilots in the opening sentences is a reason for the speaker's opinion, not evidence of other opinions. The last sentence about German people is irrelevant. This is, however, sounder than Candidate A's answer, given above, and shows an attempt to use sources.   *(L2-6)*

We are so grateful to the pilots and allied personnel. We are so happy that they help our war torn nation and capital recover and rise up and become the Germany it once was. The allies are our friends. They do not take our industry and things from our land and put it in their own like the Russians but instead add to them so we can recover. It is a true act of sincerity. They do not let the Russians dominate our people and protect us from the Communist threat. The children like the pilots because they received money and chocolate.

Fig. 5.6 Candidate B, question 2

This answer just struggles into level 2. The idea that all people in Berlin felt the same way is very important. The candidate assumes the West Berliners have short memories! The Allies had spent some years bombing Berlin flat; this appears to have been forgiven very rapidly. There is evidence of the use of the sources and some explanation of the context.   *(L2-4)*

Explain the thoughts and feelings of pilots ordered to fly supplies of coal and other materials into Berlin: 1948

Example 3

Being employed by the R.A.F. or the U.S.A.F we do not really have much choice about flying to and from Berlin. To some of us, it's just another mission which it's our job to fly but it's harder work than usual. It's also very tiring and dangerous because you have to be right on schedule because planes are landing and taking off from the same airstrip within minutes of one another. They are moving about 4000 tons of cargo a day and therefore everything has to work well. We land, unload, are cleaned and off again back for more. Its really odd to be carrying such things as coal. Some of my colleagues were amazed when they heard it, and some even said they would refuse until they realised they had to obey orders. This is worthwhile because I have heard some pilots say that we would be letting the people of Berlin down if we didn't help them. Why should the Russians control them? The organization of the zones was all settled peaceably and yet now they want to change their minds. All they would do is impose communism on the poor people of the city. Who are really having to be brave and face hardships such as having no heating, even during the winter months. It is not their fault that they are political pawns. France, Britain and America took responsibility of defending the Berliner's rights. If I were down

Continued

Continued

there I wouldn't want to be deserted. Some British pilots say, "Why bother about the Germans, leave them to the communists, they deserve that for killing so many people, my friends, relations, flattening towns and destroying as much as they could", and I would agree. But others, particularly American pilots, reply that it really wasn't, the German citizens, the children, it was members of the Nazi party. They've been rounded up and are being punished so why should their countrymen be abused further? We shouldn't let the Reds get away with it. Finally, for the west to hold Berlin puts a spoke in the Soviet wheel. It breaks down her strength quite a lot and just lately she has become strong enough to start threatening us. In a few years' time she could be very powerful and this blockade is a demonstration of her aggression.

Fig. 5.7 Candidate C, question 1

This is obviously a much more detailed and lengthy account than was the case in the previous examples, **but this fact alone does not gain access to level 3**. The crucial question when assessing this answer is, 'Is there evidence here of a range of different views held by the airmen who took part in the airlift 1948–49?' The following attitudes are brought out.

- It is our job, we just get on with it.
- We mustn't let the West Berliners down.
- We must stop the Russians–anticommunists.
- Why should we help the Germans? Let them suffer!
- Let's hold Russia up–she's getting too big and powerful.

A considerable amount of supporting detail is provided which puts this answer into a high level 3 category. *(L3-9/10)*

We were so relieved to get these supplies. When we first heard of the 'Technical Problems' which were heavily disguised as a blockade we knew that we only had enough food and fuel to last a month and a half. We were desperately worried that we would have to starve. It is fortunate that the blockade happened now in a way. With luck it will be finished by winter or we could freeze. We are so glad that we are getting aid. We've suffered so much already and we had just thought the trouble had ended. We're so thankful that the allies are not leaving us and are fighting against the Communists on our behalf, without them we could not resist. Eventually we would have to turn to the communists for things like food and then they would have control of us. I would loathe living in a communist regime, after so many years of knowing freedom, even life under Hitler seems better than living under them. For what we did to them they think we must be made to pay and I am sure that they do not, and will not hesitate to make us escape to the West. I hope the West wins, if they abandon us after a few months it will be worse for us giving in to them right now. I can only hope and pray but for now I thank the American and British forces for temporarily postponing what could be a serious situation.

Fig. 5.8 Candidate C, question 2

This is a level 2 answer, although it is quite long. It concentrates on the point of view of the writer/speaker only. There is some detail concerning why West Berliners would be grateful to the Allies. The piece contains one or two errors.

- 'Even life under Hitler seems better than living under the Russians.'
- 'The Russians will not hesitate to make us escape to the West . . .'

These show incomplete comprehension of context. *(L2-6)*

Assignment 2 World Powers since 1917(2)

Assessment testing empathy

The Berlin Question 1945–71 (continued)

Study sources **F** to **J** carefully and then answer the questions about them.

Source F: From a history textbook.

> On 13 August 1961, under the watchful eyes of the Soviet police, workmen began building the wall, completely sealing off the Eastern sector of the city.

Source G: From a history textbook.

> On 3 September 1971, a four power agreement on Berlin was reached. The USA, and the USSR, Britain and France were to remain ruling in Berlin. The links between West Berlin and West Germany were to be improved and West Berliners were to have easier access to East Berlin.

Questions

4 What private thoughts and feelings do you think the East German workmen would have had about their job of building the wall in August 1961? *(10)*

5 How might American visitors to Berlin in 1961 react if they arrived in the town just after the wall had been completed? *(10)*

Candidate A

I think the East German workmen would have felt terrible about building the wall because they were stopping people from getting to their jobs and homes and families. It must have been like building their own prison, they were free to walk the streets but could not see their family.

Fig. 5.9 Candidate A, question 4

This is a level 1 answer for the same reasons given for Candidate A's question 2. The candidate imagines what it would be like being cut off by the wall, but the answer is so short and undeveloped that there is no chance of showing a progression from everyday empathy to stereotyped empathy. The results of the wall (being cut off from jobs and family, and lacking freedom) are well expressed. *(L1-3)*

This candidate did not attempt question 4 so scored 0.

Total mark $= \frac{3}{20} = \frac{1.5}{10}$

This shows the importance of completing all coursework tasks. You must be careful in timed exercises to 'pace' yourself—do not let yourself spend too long on one section so that you are unable to finish the questions.

This was done with Assignment 1 as a combined assignment.

So, for candidate A, the total mark $= 4 + 2 + 3 + 0 = \frac{9}{40}$

I dare not tell any more of this as I am afraid that I will be imprisoned or maybe shot. Why do they make us build a wall through the heart of Germany. They are splitting up a race of people who have been together through many wars and it is hurting its pride by making the people of Germany building it. My friends are saying they work on the wall for a job and would do anything to get into the West and not be trapped behind a wall which I consider will be up for a long time. They could at least try to brighten it up. It could put people off coming to visit the city because they will see the wall.

Fig. 5.10 Candidate B, question 5

This is a sound level 2 answer. There is a brief hint of **differentiated empathy** but the 'friends' mentioned apparently were all of the same view. Some contextual inaccuracy: the Germans had certainly been split before (at least once of their own doing!) and the reference to the brightness of the walls is hardly a key point. Nor was the effect on tourism to Berlin a particularly valuable observation. *(L2-5)*

The wall is a bit of an eyesore isn't it? The guards, machine guns, observation platforms, minefields, barbed wire and graffitti do nothing to enhance it. It is also a great pity that all the houses within 200 metres of the wall have been emptied and left derelict, but I suppose thats politics. At least now we can keep the communists out if there is an emergency by using the wall. It does not allow us to explore the east German side.

Fig. 5.11 Candidate B, question 4

This is a good example of a level 1 answer. It is an illustration of what happens when a candidate is running out of time in a timed exercise. The answer is mainly descriptive and little mention is made of attitudes of visitors, as required by the question. *(L1-2)*

This candidate has produced a much more solid answer paper than has Candidate A. The answers show a more detailed knowledge and display a greater understanding than those of Candidate A. Some use is made of the sources which receives credit. Clearly, however, the candidate did not pace him/herself and wrote one or two short answers.

Thus for Candidate B the total mark $= 6+4+5+2 = \frac{17}{40}$

Candidate C

As an East German workman building the wall in 1961, I think that regardless of whether I was for or against the communist system in which I live and work, I think that I would feel very bitter towards the thing that I was constructing. It is one thing which would finally resign the East Germans to the fact that they were under the control of Russia and there was no way to get out and the very fact that they were being made to build the very thing which symbolised the taking away of their liberty must have annoyed them. Not only would there be a terrible sense of frustration and despair at digging ones own grave each time you put more mortar on top of another you were physically splitting up families, possibly your own. To sever the bonds of love yourself, to be forced into that position by the Russians who could just as well have built it to spare the Germans would make me for ever bitter towards them. The wall could be seperating me from my family, friends and even my job. It took away my only hope of freedom and free life ever again. I would become very jealous of the people on the other side of the wall and I would really want to be one of them. It is also possible that I could hate the work itself and it would be easy to feel

Continued

completely helpless and deserted by the allies, who, in agreeing the sectors with Russia condemned you just as much to this as they did. Then again it is possible that I wasn't aware of the implications of the wall and presumed that it would not make much difference to the way that life had continued before. I would only find out in the weeks to follow the things it had denied me.

Fig. 5.12 Candidate C, question 3

Another level 2 answer, putting across one view only. There are no obvious errors of understanding.   (L2-7)

The American visitors would probably be dumbfounded at this novel creation. Some of them would probably also be quite annoyed at the prospect of not being able, without a lot of running around, to obtain the necessary visas and permission to see half the city they had specifically come to see. After the initial shock they would be very curious about it and would probably visit the wall itself and enquire as to how and why it came to be put there. If they received a satisfactory answer I would imagine that some of them would start to get very angry and resentful. I think questions such as 'What right have they got to be there?', or 'What right have they got to build this wall?' would be asked. It would be quite likely that one or two American visitors would be Communists, or at least sympathetic to the Left. They would defend the building of the wall, saying the Russians had every right to build a wall in their own zone, and that it was only necessary to keep out evil influences from the West.

Those who were not particularly interested in politics would very probably excitedly tell stories in their letters or postcards to their friends back home about the monstrosity. Some might be genuinely worried by the gesture from the East to the West. These may have considered the horrendous possibilities of hostilities between Russia and the U.S.A., as well as feeling sympathy for the other side. They might also have felt a sense of security from being in the West as well as a silent threat from the wall and the land behind it. Most of the visitors may have felt a sense of national outrage as they may have felt it was a gesture aimed directly at America.

Fig. 5.13 Candidate C, question 4

This is a very clear level 3 answer. The candidate demonstrates a wide range of views and, very important, adds accurate detail in context to support the answer.   *(L3-10)*

$$\text{Total} = \frac{17}{20} = \frac{8.5}{10}$$

In the combined assessment this candidate scored a total of

$$9 + 6 + 7 + 10 = \frac{32}{40}$$

This candidate's work reveals a highly developed sense of **empathetic understanding**.

Summary

It will be evident to you that there is a great deal of difference in the work of these candidates. However their answers have only been assessed on their understanding of the content of empathy and their ability to place this in context. They have not been penalized for poor grammar or spelling.

Your work should not be penalized for poor grammar or spelling.

You may also have noticed that the candidates, on two occasions, had not read the question correctly. For example, question 3 asks for the thoughts and feelings of **workmen** yet two of the answers were given as though from *one* person. You should look out for clues in the wording of the questions in empathy assignments as well as in assignments testing skills in handling sources.

1 The skill of **empathy** or the ability to **empathize** is important in the study of history, and has become an integral part of the GCSE syllabus.

2 Empathy is not simply putting yourself in the place of an individual or a group of people in an historical context. It demands greater skill and an all round historical knowledge of the period in question.

Marks can be lost by not reading the question properly.

3 Empathy assignments provide the opportunity to display an awareness of the ways in which other people and societies differ from your own.

4 You will be required to relate your points of view and feelings towards specific historical situations.

5 Answers must be based on clear, real, historical evidence and knowledge.

6 An empathy answer is *not* just a piece of imaginary writing.

7 Remember, empathy assessments are written as though *you* were placed *back* in time. It is not written *now*, looking back.

Individual study

Don't be put off reading this section if you are not doing an individual study. The tips and hints here apply to other coursework as well.

Some examination groups allow candidates to submit individual historical studies as part of their coursework. The restriction, if any, on subject matter and the number of words you have to write for the study needs to be discussed with your teacher as early as possible in the course, to give you plenty of time to complete it. Some groups allow the use of material other than the written word, such as sound or video tapes, as part of the project. This would also need to be clarified.

Time management is vital when doing an individual study.

The writing up of your completed study will be done in your own home, or maybe at school, but the research involved before you write it will require you to do some work **in the field**, or in other words outside your home or classroom, for example, at museums, historical sites, record offices etc. This means that you will have to set aside some of your own free time in which to collect material.

It is very important to remember that history may not be the only individual study you are doing. The planning of your time is vital and you must take into consideration not **only** your individual studies but **also** the completion dates for coursework assignments in all subjects!

Choosing a topic

If you have done classroom projects before you have probably been given the title by your teacher but the actual content has been left up to you. In GCSE courses the title could be your own choice as well, so what do you need to consider?

The danger with **free-choice** individual studies is that you may tend to be too ambitious and choose titles which are too wide in scope—for example, 'The History of Nursing', 'The development of Fashion from 1500 to 1988', 'The Horse in History'. Studies of this nature cover too large an area, and the completed work will be superficial and provide only a limited amount of information. So what do you need to consider when choosing your title?

Remember you will be under a lot of pressure for time and you may have individual studies to do for other subjects, so you need to choose a topic which will be relatively easy to complete. For instance, if you live in the south of England it would be inconvenient for you to study the history of an area or a village in Scotland or Northern Ireland. You may be tempted to try this because you have relatives in the area who could provide you with the information you need, but you should be *very wary* of carrying out your study in this way. Your plans would rely on the other person's organization, over which you have no control. You would not be doing the work yourself, and the point of an examination individual study is to give the candidate the experience of being a practical historian.

You also need to choose a topic for which there is a reasonable amount of resource material available for general use. To satisfy the course requirements you will have to provide evidence that you have used some **primary sources** (see page 66). Some topics, such as those devoted to an historical character, lend themselves to the use of **secondary source** material only. All you have to do in such a case is find a number of relevant books on the subject, note the facts from them and use these accordingly.

What you need is a project which:
- does not include a lot of travelling from your home to the study area
- has a reasonable amount of primary source material available
- is relatively simple to research
- does not cover too large a subject area, and yet is enjoyable to research and of interest to anyone reading it.

'Choose a project which you will find interesting to study.'

Choose something which you enjoy doing. You may have to spend a lot of time researching your facts so it must **interest** you.

If you are also doing an individual study for another subject, such as geography, it would be worth looking at the possibility of choosing project titles which are compatible so that you may be able to do the research for both at the same time. For example, if you chose to do the historical development of a local village you could also research its geographical location and its influence on the site's geographical development.

Having chosen your title, after full consultation with your teacher, where do you start?

The next Section covers the way in which you can extract documents from your local record office, but before you get that far in your research you need to be properly equipped.

You will need to take some basic equipment with you when doing research in the field. A pen is useful, but a sharp pencil is **vital**. Most libraries and record offices allow researchers to use only pencils when taking notes, so that they do not get ink on valuable documents and manuscripts. Do not forget that you will also require a pencil sharpener! A notebook is essential, and if it is small enough to fit into your pocket so much the better. Some people prefer to work on sheets of paper which can be stored in a file. There is nothing wrong with this method, indeed it does have some advantages because you can file similar material together. However, it is also easy to lose the odd sheet which can be very annoying when you come to write up your field notes.

A camera could be useful for any local project, not only to produce illustrations for the final study but also to provide you with photographs which could remind you of what you saw during your visit. Do not forget that you may need permission to take photographs inside churches and public buildings and some establishments charge a fee!

Whenever you are working outside always carry a medium-sized clear plastic bag in your pocket; if it rains you can continue to use your notebook inside the bag. If you go out specifically to make some sketches, it is always advisable to clip the paper to a board to give it support.

Portable tape recorders are useful because they allow you to record spoken information in full, to be written out later at home. This does not only apply to interviewing people. It is also useful for you when looking at an area. You can describe it in detail, and even read out inscriptions or significant facts from plaques, without having to write them down. Remember, if you interview people it is polite to **ask permission** to record their answers on tape rather than assume that they will not mind.

Before you make any journey into the field you will need to plan very carefully how you will use the time. This could save you making many journeys to the same place and avoid the frustration of not having the correct information to hand.

Having decided on the title for your individual study you will now have to decide how to present it. How it has to be finally submitted for marking will be laid down by the examination group but you still need to plan your project in as much detail as possible. The plan needs to be flexible so that you can add any new ideas or information which you find during your research.

For writing up field notes and for your final submission always work on file paper so that any additional information can be slotted in at the relevant point.

If you plan your project before you begin writing, it could save you a lot of time later on. It can help you plan visits and what you want to gain from them. It also helps to put your rough notes into some sort of order. It is worth spending a lot of time writing possible chapter and subheadings, with their contents, and then moving them around until they form the basis of a well-structured individual study.

One of the most popular historical studies is one which looks at the historical development of a settlement, or part of a settlement. Below is a list of guidelines which may help you when investigating such an area. Some of the suggestions apply equally well to other topics.

Guidelines

A settlement study

1 It is more convenient to select a study area which is easily accessible from your home. Therefore it needs to be on a public transport route (bus or train), or within easy cycling or walking distance. Consequently, the easiest place to study is the district in which you live, or, alternatively, around the home of a relative with whom you could stay.

2 Because most of the work for this project will be carried out in the field and in the local library and record office, it is best to set aside a specific period of time in which to complete your initial investigations. A few weeks of the school holiday would be ideal. Remember, weekends may not always be convenient because most reference libraries are closed; there may not be a bus service to the area at a weekend and some of the features you particularly wish to study may not be available.

3 Your project needs to be well planned before you start gathering material. A few minutes of planning could save you hours of wasted time and energy, having to visit a place for a second or third time to collect information you should have gathered on the first visit. Check early closing days for shops and the most convenient time for visiting churches and any other public buildings.

A settlement offers many different opportunities for a local study.

4 At this planning stage you need to decide whether you are going to study the village by looking at it today and investigating the causes of its present situation, or whether you are going to start at its earliest known beginnings and trace its chronological development to the present day. It would be easier to do the latter as a series of patches at specific periods during its history, or when some external factors, such as The Civil War, 1642–46, have played an important part in its development. You may also decide to study the village through the experience of a particular family, or group of families, or the influence of an important industry such as coal mining or textile mills, on the settlement.

5 When gathering information for a general village study remember to concentrate on its historical development and include as many aspects of its life as possible, both in the past and in the present. For example, try to include examples of the following:

- a study of the early history of the village using any available archaeological evidence you may have found

- a general explanation of the physical development of the community by investigating the general history of the buildings; use available clues to date the buildings and make a **trend-line** of the line of settlement

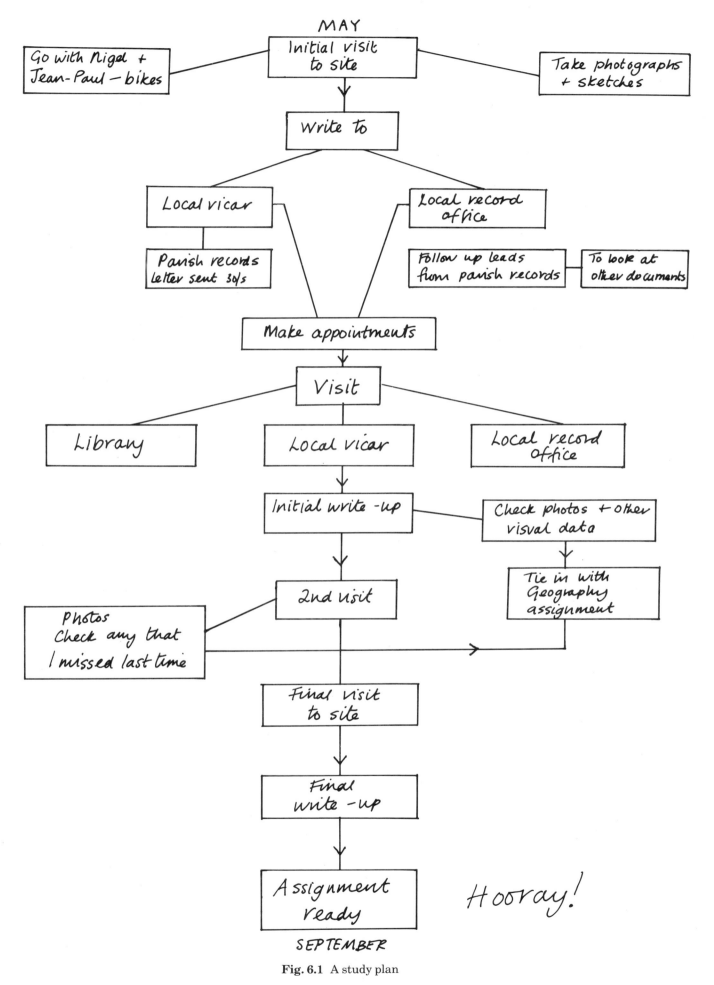

Fig. 6.1 A study plan

- something of the history of individual buildings such as the church, manor house or school, or any feature that may be unusual in some way, such as a folly or memorial

- a study of an individual family or group of families on the history of the settlement

- the influence of a particular trade or industry.

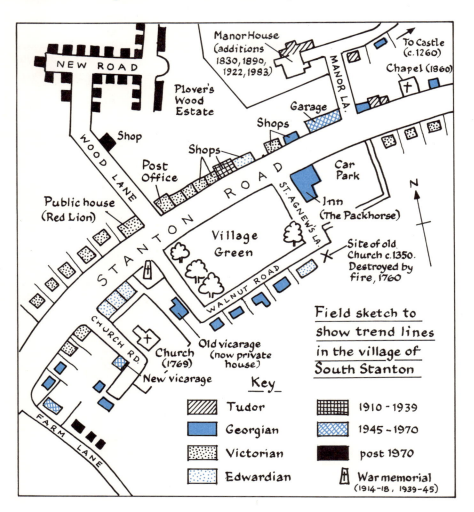

Fig. 6.2 A trend-line

6 A settlement study does give you more opportunity to study your own individual interests. As well as the suggestions above, you could limit your study to individual aspects of village life. For example you could look at the life of a servant employed in the 'big house', rectory or similar building in your area at certain times in history. Or you could investigate the life of a farm or forest labourer on the local estate, or a worker in the local factory, especially if a particular company was and perhaps still *is* an important employer in the community. A study such as this would be useful if you were following a social and economic course in the classroom.

7 Remember your project has to be presented in as neat a way as possible. (Section Seven covers this in detail.) Do not waste a great deal of research by poor presentation.

8 When you introduce your study remember to show, on maps, both the area's **general** and **specific** location in the country. As with all work, make all your maps and diagrams as neat as possible, and include a title, key and scale (if applicable). Each picture or photograph should have a title and the date it was drawn or taken. Any annotations or labels should be written horizontally.

Visual material

Not all examination boards require a written submission for an individual study. It may be possible for you to include sound, film, photographic or video material. These require different skills of presentation and interpretation and before you embark on such a course you need to discuss your ideas in detail with your teacher.

Your own photographs can form a useful part of any study and they are reasonably easy to include. So, too, can sound recordings if they are interviews or observations which you have recorded during your research. However, it would be very difficult to base a complete study on these recordings without doing some written work to explain their significance. They should perhaps be considered in the same way as your own photographic evidence—as an integral part of a project rather than the sole resource for it.

Where photographs can provide the basis for a complete study is when you are able to use archive photographs of an area or event and either compare them with later pictures taken from the same point or use them to discuss **witting** and **unwitting** testimony (see Section Ten).

What you need to do when looking at any photograph is to look beyond the obvious subject matter and examine the background detail. As with any other source material, photographs should be treated with care. You are seeing another person's view of the subject matter, so in this respect it must be **biased**. Remember also that archive photographs were limited by the equipment being used and early examples were often 'staged'. Bear this in mind when using them.

Photographs useful for reference for individual studies can usually be seen at local reference libraries or museums. One obvious source is a history textbook.

Archive 'moving' film needs to be treated in a different way and you need to consider the difficulties its use can create before attempting to use it in any study. Archive film is very difficult to see unless you go to places such as the Imperial War Museum, which has daily showings of archive film on aspects of warfare and social history pertaining to it.

Another source is the television. Programmes are often devoted to archive film and it may be possible to get a video of these from your local distributor. However, it is unlikely that you will be able to find film that is directly related to the topic you are studying. Therefore because of lack of time you really must consider whether moving film is a necessary requirement for your study. It would perhaps be more useful just as another resource but you still need a few simple guidelines.

Before you see any film, and you may have to travel a long way to do so, you need to know what it is about and whether or not it will be useful. You should also have a reasonable understanding of the general history of the times in which the film was taken, the subject of the film and, if possible, why it was made.

You will also find that is can be difficult to take notes from moving film, unless you are using a video where you can stop or pause the film. Otherwise, the best thing to do is write down a general impression of the facts contained in the film. There is no need to write down all the details because in early films much, if not all, of the film was shot from the same place. Once you have a general impression of the film you can then concentrate on the unwitting testimony which may be of more use to you. Remember, as with still photographs, you are only seeing the cameraman's view of the situation, so again you must be wary of biased filming.

If you are really keen to use film, an unusual individual study would be one where you actually made a video film and put on a soundtrack to explain what it is about. This would have to include some detailed historical information about the area being filmed. A lot of research would still have to be done beforehand but it would certainly be an unusual and rewarding study.

To sum up As you can see, you need to put a lot of preliminary work and thought into your individual study before you even put pen to paper. This planning is vital if you are to use your limited time wisely and effectively. Remember, you need to consult your teacher and seek advice *at all stages*.

Checklist

1 If you decide to do an individual study as part of your GCSE you should discuss the idea with your teacher as early as possible.

2 An individual study will require you to work in the field.

3 It is **vital** that you plan your use of time well. History may not be the only subject which requires an individual study.

4 Remember you will also have to allow time to do coursework assignments.

5 Do not be too ambitious with your title, otherwise the finished study will be too superficial.

6 Things to consider when choosing a title include:

- you will be under a lot of time pressure so you need to be able to complete it easily
- make sure your study or study area is convenient and easily accessible
- your study needs sufficient resource material
- make sure your research facilities are easily accessible
- choose a topic you will *enjoy doing*.

7 If you are doing other individual studies check with your teachers to see if there are titles which are compatible.

8 Basic equipment required for field work should include:

- pen
- pencil
- pencil sharpener
- notebook
- camera
- clipboard
- portable tape recorder if you are doing interviews or recording your own observations.

9 Remember, you may have to seek permission before taking photographs in churches or other public buildings.

10 Spend time sorting out a rough plan of your ideas before your start your study. This plan should be as flexible as possible.

11 All photographic illustrative and map material included in your project should be well presented and labelled.

12 If you decide to produce a study based on audio, video or photographic material you need to seek advice from your teacher before you start.

Presentation of individual studies

It is very important to present your work in as neat a way as possible, whether it is an individual study or a written assignment. Although you will not lose marks for poor presentation, the work does have to be read and understood by your teacher when it is being assessed.

This section examines how best to present an individual study and looks at the ways in which you can improve your written answers for your coursework assignments.

Guidelines The number of words, if it is purely a written study, or restrictions on the use of other material which may be used should be discussed with your teacher *before* you start research for your study. However you decide to present your material, there are guidelines which you need to take into account before handing it in and which, if adhered to, will make your individual study look worthy of all the work you would have put into it.

Some of the following points will not necessarily apply to your particular study but most of the guidelines are applicable in a general way, not only to history studies but also to other subjects as well.

1 Your individual study should have a relevant **title** on a separate page. Remember, this title may have to be chosen and agreed some time **before** you complete the study, so make sure you keep a copy of the title you discussed with your teacher. If you wish to make any changes ask for advice before doing so.

2 If your handwriting is neat, you can write the project in ink. (Some groups may insist on this, so make sure you check with your teacher.) If, however, your handwriting is untidy and you have access to a typewriter or a word-processor and you are confident in using one, then this is a better way to present your written material. Do not use a ball-point pen, especially if you are writing on both sides of the paper, because you will find that the pressure of the ball will come through on the other side and spoil the look of the work.

3 If you have divided your work into **chapters**, each one should have a **title**. So too should pictures, photographs, diagrams, charts and any other illustrations you might include.

4 If possible, write a **contents page** at the beginning of the study and include a very brief **summary** of what each chapter contains.

5 You can use colour to distinguish certain features and aspects of your study, such as statistical diagrams, maps and sketches, but do not use felt-tip pens for colouring for two reasons:

- the ink in felt-tip pens can be thick, especially when covering a large area, so if you use them on a map or diagram you may obscure some of the important written details beneath the shading

- felt-pen ink tends to soak through pages, which means that the other side cannot be written on and it looks untidy and will detract from your study.

6 Use coloured pencil for all shading. Do not use wax crayons. Do not colour too heavily because, again, this will obscure the fine detail. You need to give only a suggestion of colour, so shade very lightly.

7 Always shade in the same direction.

8 If you draw any pie charts or other statistical diagrams such as block graphs, always highlight the divisions between sections, using a ruler and a very fine pen.

9 It is very important to **label** all the **axes** on graphs and statistical diagrams. Use a **key** if this will make the diagram clearer. A key should **always** be included on any map. A **scale** and **direction pointer** would also be useful.

10 Include a list of all the books, pamphlets, papers etc that you have used in your study.

11 Always acknowledge those people who have helped you with your study. Especially acknowledge those who have allowed you access to specific documents or have helped you in other ways.

12 While you are writing your study, keep it in a file so that any additional information can be added to it at a later date.

13 Remember that you may not get your photographs or documents back so it would be worthwhile, and perhaps necessary, to make photocopies of any documents you include, especially if they are not yours. Include **copies** of photographs whenever possible. Do not include **any** original copies of primary source material.

14 Make sure you know the date by which your individual study or your coursework assignment has to be completed. It would be a great pity if your work was not assessed because it was handed in too late!

Study skills

'Extra reading at home will help you gain an understanding of the topic.'

You should have noticed by now that to gain high marks in your coursework you need to have a good **background knowledge** of the topic being assessed. This information can be gained from your classroom lessons, but extra reading at home would **certainly** be an advantage. You do not need to read a great amount but you do need to be selective; in other words read only what is relevant. For example to gain information on the events of 'Crystal Night 1938' (also known as *Kristallnacht* or 'the Night of the Broken Glass') would not require you to read the complete history of the Third Reich!

For details of events, or individuals, you need to use the **index** at the back of a book dealing with the period in question. The entries will almost certainly be listed in alphabetical order. All you have to do is find the topic you require in the index and read the page number(s) listed alongside it in order to find where the topic is discussed in the book.

Suppose you need to find out what role Reich-Marshal Goering played in the events of the previous example, 'Crystal Night 1938'. You could first find a biography of Goering in the school or local library: *The Reich-Marshal* by Leonard Mosely, published by Weidenfeld & Nicolson would be a useful reference. Turn to the index at the back of the book and look at the entries under 'C', (or 'K' for *Kristallnacht*, or 'N' for 'Night of the Broken Glass'), until you come across a reference to 'Crystal Night'. If it is not there at all you will have to search in another book. However, in this case the index entry is as follows:

"Crystal Night," 228, 243 – 44.

You now know that you can find the information you require on page 228 and on pages 243 – 44. All you need do then is read these pages and collect the details. You have not had to read the complete book! You can use this same method for any topic you are studying.

Taking notes

Having found the information how do you remember it?

Notes from books

One of the most important skills an historian requires is the ability to read a piece of writing, or examine a specific document or photograph and extract the details and facts from it. Having found your references to 'Crystal Night' you will need to take notes from them.

But why take notes?

It is very difficult to retain information from written evidence just by reading it. Try a simple test. How much detail can you remember from the last few novels, or even magazine articles, that you have read? In this case if you cannot remember anything it does not really matter, but if you were reading books for your school work it could be very important to remember the facts. You may need to use them in 18 months' time! Without making notes while you are reading a passage you are unlikely to remember the facts, especially if you are using more than one book covering the same topic.

A great deal of what you read in any study is irrelevant for your particular research. By extracting notes you are identifying only those facts relevant to the topic and you are therefore ignoring all the details that are of no use to you. When you come to read these notes at a later date they will save you a lot of time in extra research and you will know that they are relevant and useful to your study.

Notes are therefore useful in three ways:

1 As an aid to the memory in recalling details from a passage.

2 As an aid to concentrating the mind on what you are reading at the time you take the notes.

3 Saving time in the future when it comes to revision or the need to re-read the topic.

There are many different methods of taking notes. These are a matter of individual choice and, as you will see in the examples below, the style may depend on the type of source material being used. Whatever method you use, make sure that your notes can be read and understood at any time, as sometimes you may not be able to refer back to the original source.

Before you start making notes it is very important to write down the source of the information. Whenever possible this should include the title, author's name, publisher, the 'Dewey' reference number (see Section Nine) and where the book can be found again, if you need it e.g. school library, public library etc.

It is also very important to make sure any notes you make are relevant to the topic.

Making notes does not mean copying out large chunks of text. Notes are often written down in a form of shorthand, to save both time and space. Everyone has a different style of taking notes. You will soon be able to work out your own form of shorthand but do not forget—however you take notes or shorten words you *must* be able to understand them later. If you use initials in your notes you need to remember what they mean. However, if a sentence is so well written or relevant to your study that you cannot reduce or paraphrase it then copy it out, put it into quotation marks and use it as a quotation. If you do this you must acknowledge it, either by putting the author's name in brackets afterwards or by referring to it in another way, e.g. As Thompson says; 'In this conjunction of circumstances . . . lies the most fundamental explanation of why the First World War broke out', or, 'The war which broke out in 1914 . . . was in many ways novel in human history.' (Thompson)

Example

You have been given the following information about the life of a domestic servant in Edwardian England and you are required to take notes on it in order to answer a question on the 'Life of a Kitchen maid in 1910'. As in most cases it is important to read the complete passage first before taking any notes in order to obtain a broader idea of the details the passage contains.

> The kitchen maid's first duty after the fire is lighted is to sweep and clear the kitchen and the offices belonging to it. This she does every morning, besides cleaning the stone steps at the entrance of the house, the front door step, the halls, the passages and the stairs, if any, which lead to the kitchen. Her general duties, besides, are to wash and scour all these places twice a week and the tables, shelves and cupboards. She also has to attend to the nursery and servants' hall dinners while they are cooking, to prepare all fish, poultry and vegetables, to trim meat joints and cutlets and all work the cook may assign to her. In short the duties of the kitchen maid are to assist the cook and keep the kitchen and all the kitchen utensils clean.

When at work all the staff should dress suitably: short dresses, well-fitting boots, and overalls or large aprons with bibs, of which every cook and kitchen maid should have a good supply. Staff will then be comfortable as they can never be with long dresses, small aprons and slipshod shoes. All staff should be neat and tidy.

A typical work routine of a small house containing one or two servants, including the kitchen maid, would be as follows:

Monday: Home washing.

Tuesday: Sweeping and cleaning of servants' bedrooms and one or two other rooms and stairs cleaned to the lower floor.

Wednesday: The sweeping and cleaning of the best bedrooms and all the windows.

Thursday: Cleaning and turning out of cupboards and cleaning of passages and stairs.

Friday: Sweeping and cleaning of drawing room and cleaning silver.

Saturday: Sweeping and cleaning of dining room and kitchen including coppers.

Mrs Beeton's All About Cookery, Ward Lock & Co., 1920

What notes would you extract from this passage? Take notes from it now, then see if yours correspond to those below.

Life of Kitchen Maid 1910. Source: 'Mrs Beeton's All about Cooking' Ward Lock & Co. 1920

a. 1st duty, after fire lit: Sweep, clear kitch. offices every morn. + clean stove, front steps, halls, passages + stairs to kitch.

b. General dut: wash + scour all these twice a wk. + tables, shelves + cupboards.

c. Attend to nursery + servants dinn.

d. Prepare all fish, poultry + veg.

e. Trim meat, cutlets + work for cook.

GEN: Assist cook, keep kitch. + utensils clean.

DRESS: Short dress, good boots, overalls/ large apron with bib – should have good supply.

TYPICAL ROUTINE (+ above)

Mon. Home washing

Tues. Sweep/ clean serv. bed + 1/2 other rooms + all stairs.

Wed. Sw/cl best bed. + all windows.

Thurs. Cl. all passages + stairs + turn out all cupboards.

Fri. Sw/cl drawing rm. + clean silver.

Sat. Sw/cl dining rm, kitch + coppers.

Fig. 8.1 Note-taking

The notes in Figure 8.1 contain all the relevant information from the passage which would be useful when you are answering the question. The notes are short and concise but they are still easily understood.

Taking notes from photographic evidence

We have concentrated on taking notes from written source material. During your period of study you are certain to use other types of resources. Often photographic and documentary evidence is required and the details contained in these also have to be noted in some way.

One way of noting photographic evidence is by the use of **annotation**.

If the photograph is **your own property** or you have been **given** a photocopy of one in the lesson, you can stick it onto a larger piece of card or paper and then draw lines from the important details on the picture to the margin around the outside and write your notes there. These notes, or labels, are the annotations. Remember to write all the notes **horizontally** to make sure they can be read from one direction without having to turn the page around! Do not let the lines indicating the position of the annotations cross, otherwise they become very confusing. The neater the notes the easier they will be to understand at a later date.

The method above is fine if you are able to keep the photograph or a copy but what happens if the photograph is in a book? In this case the notes you take will need to be understood without the help of the picture.

If you are unable to use the photograph itself, then the best method is to make a simple sketch of it. You do not need to be a great artist to do this. You will be interested in the picture for a particular reason, therefore you will be able to leave out any of the details that are not relevant.

You may only need to sketch a small part of it. You are not aiming to produce a work of art; in fact the simpler you make your drawing, the simpler it will be to understand later on. Once you have made your sketch you simply annotate it in the same way as described before. Some pictures will be more difficult to sketch than others but it is a simple skill to master.

Another way of retaining information is to trace the picture. To protect the original, **always** cover it with a thin sheet of plastic or glass. It does not matter what you use as long as you can see through it and you do not harm the picture by pressing too hard onto it. Simply lay the material onto the picture, put a piece of tracing paper onto this and then copy the section you need. This method can be very useful when you need to identify individuals within a group photograph. All you need to do is trace around the heads of the people and put their names on the outlines.

Notes from other sources

During your GCSE course in school you will be provided with information in a number of different ways. It will come in the form of:

- written information in books
- written information on the blackboard or overhead projector
- the spoken word from a teacher as an explanation or as a commentary to a film, film-strip or other visual material
- information spoken on a sound or video-tape
- a combination of all four.

There are two sorts of notes you can take from a blackboard. Your teacher may say, 'Copy down all these points into your books,' or, 'In your own words copy down the most important points from the information on the board.'

The difference is that in the first statement you are expected to copy down the facts on the board word for word, and in the second you have been given the option of writing the same details in your own words, and only those which you consider to be important.

Even if you are copying facts from the board you still need to be able to remember them clearly because they will be an important part of your coursework. You may find it easier to use different colours to highlight the most important details, or to underline the dates, names and events which you particularly want to remember or which are a vital part of the topic.

> *Coloured pens can be useful for highlighting important points.*

Taking notes from the spoken word is a much more difficult skill and one which requires practice. The problem is that unlike a tape or video recorder, they cannot be switched off or 'paused'. Even if you are listening to a tape or watching a video you are usually not in control of it. Therefore what you have to try to do is develop your own form of shorthand writing, even more brief than the abbreviations you may use in your written notes, and to take the notes as quickly as possible as the person is speaking or a tape is playing. There will obviously be occasions when you miss a certain point so always take advantage of any time when the teacher may ask 'Are there any questions?' Gathering and understanding the facts are vital to your course so do not feel too embarrassed to ask your teacher to go over a point again.

This shorthand skill is worth developing. Practise it by taking notes from any television programme. What you must remember to do with class notes is to put them into some sort of **order** as soon as possible after the lesson, while the topic is still fresh in your mind and, while reading them, you can recall the other details you did not have time to write down.

 **Checklist**

1 Remember that you may not need these notes for some time after you have written them so they must be:

- reasonably neat
- legible
- easily understood.

2 At school you are likely to write and store your notes in an exercise book. If you are working **in the field**, i.e. in museums or on trips most of your notes will be on pads, or on paper clipped to a simple clip-board. Whatever you write them on **all** notes must be kept safely!

3 It is always useful to put a date on your notes and also to record where they were taken from. You must always note the title of any written source, and where possible the author and publisher so that you can locate the source again should you wish to do so.

4 Some notes will be used almost immediately especially if you have written them with a particular title or piece of coursework in mind. Others may not be required until your final examination, perhaps in 18 months' time. Therefore it is very important to follow the procedure highlighted in **3** above.

5 Your notes are a shortened version of what you have seen, heard or read. So, in some cases, when you come to use them you may simply have to fill in the missing words.

6 You need to develop your own method of taking shorthand notes from the spoken word. Then practise it until you become proficient.

7 Notes from photographic/pictorial evidence can be written in the form of annotations on the actual article or on a copy/sketch.

Collecting data

If you are doing an individual study as part of your GCSE course you are certain to use some kind of **secondary sources** and perhaps even some **primary examples**.

Sources

Primary and secondary sources

A primary source is one which provides the historian with the information **first-hand**. It is in its original form and has not been changed since being written down, carved, drawn, painted or photographed. A primary source is also one which was produced during the event or period under investigation.

Secondary sources are simply those which provide the historian with the details **second-hand**. A researcher can go to the local record office and collect information on his local area. He then uses this information to write a book. This book is published and another person wishing to find out about the same area goes to the local library, takes the book from the shelf, reads the relevant sections and then takes notes from it. The information is now second-hand and is therefore a secondary source.

Many of the history books you use at school are secondary sources. The authors have researched the original material and documents (primary sources) and have interpreted and rewritten the information contained in them in a way the reader will understand. Authors use secondary as well as primary material and you should do the same in your study.

History books are extremely important tools for the historian. However, it is useful to remember that when you use any history book you are reading the **author's interpretation** of the facts and details available to him. This interpretation may be very one-sided or biased so, whenever possible, it is always worth reading as many books on the same topic as possible. You will find that some authors are more biased than others and some actually disagree with each other! Some may also have used, innocently or inadvertently, primary source material which itself was biased.

The type of book your choose to use will depend entirely on the individual study or assignment you are doing. Before you start detailed reading of a particular topic it is always worth 'reading around' it in order to find background information. In coursework assignments this will already have been done in the classroom, but if you are doing an individual study you will have to search for this yourself. Having read around the subject you then need to specialize.

The simplest way is to find a book dealing only with the subject matter you are interested in. The author would have researched the topic in detail so such a book should provide you with a lot of useful material.

Another method is to find books which deal with the characters who took part in an historical event linked to your work. For this you would need to find a biography or, in the case of a recent historical event, an autobiography, the difference being that an autobiography is written by the subject of the book. Do not forget that biographies, and *especially* autobiographies, can be very biased.

Books that are of little use to you are 'historical novels'. Although they may be based on historical events they *are* only stories and should be treated as such. You should *not* use them in any serious study.

Using a library

During the research for an individual study, or when you are gathering information for a piece of coursework, you are certain to need access to secondary resources so we will concentrate on how to use a library effectively. (You are unlikely to have much time to search for primary evidence. This is covered briefly at the end of this Section.)

The first problem to overcome is how to find the book you require among all those on the shelf! In small school libraries you may find that a simple code has been used in order to identify different subject areas or authors. This could be a colour code, e.g. a red label will be stuck to the spine of all books dealing with history, or they could be identified by small cartoon pictures. This may be very useful in a small library but would be unworkable in a large library containing many books. So how do you find the book you want?

Finding what you want

Imagine your library is like your local supermarket. All the items dealing with a similar sort of food can be found on shelves close to one another in the same area of the store. A library works in the same way. It is divided up into many sections all containing different subjects or subdivisions of subjects. The type of book you look for will depend on the amount of detail you are hoping to find in it! If you wish to find some general information about a certain historical event you could look first in the section marked **general reference**. This is the section which usually contains books such as dictionaries or encyclopaedias. If, for example, you were asked a question about the date of the first Cooperative movement in Rochdale you would find the answer (in this case the answer is 1844) more quickly by looking for it in an encylopaedia rather than looking through all the relevant books in the history section.

Usually an encyclopaedia is divided up into different volumes. The initial letters of the subjects contained in each volume are usually found on the spine of the individual book. All the entries are listed in alphabetical order so our answer could be found either under 'R' for Rochdale Pioneers, or 'C' for Cooperative movement.

You will not be able to remove reference books from the library, you may only refer to them in the building. However, you should be able to get the information you need quickly. Reference books are not meant to be read from cover to cover and the titles of subject areas are easily found. Sometimes a many-volumed encyclopaedia will have a separate index volume and this will give you the number of the volume and the page on which the information can be found.

Fiction books in libraries will almost certainly be sorted on the shelf in alphabetical order using the authors' surnames. For your studies you are more likely to use **non-fiction** books; these are classified in a different way. They are arranged on the shelves according to the subject matter they contain. They are *not* classified in alphabetical order.

Classification of books

Many libraries use a method known as the **Dewey Decimal Classification System**, named after an American called Melvin Dewey who divided all knowledge into **ten** parts.

This method of classification uses a series of numbers which can be found on the spine of the book as well as on the corresponding shelves containing them. The numbers range from 000–999. As an historian you would be interested in the '900s'. This covers all books dealing with history, geography and biography.

Each of the ten main sections are subdived into ten further parts so the 900s would be divided into sections 910–990 and include the following subject areas:

900: geography, history and biography
910: ancient history and archaeology
920: biography
930: general history of the ancient world
940: European history
950: general history of Asia
960: general history of Africa
970: history of North America
980: general history of South America
990: general history of other parts of the world

Sometimes you will find a decimal point and then another number after the main one, which helps to classify the books in even more detail. As you can see from the list above if you were interested in the general history of Europe, you would look for a book with the number 940 on its spine. However, because the subject area is so vast it is subdivided even further:

940.1: the history of Medieval Europe 476–1453
940.2: the history of Europe 1453–1914
940.3: the causes of World War One
940.4: the military history of World War One
940.5: the history of 20th century Europe

This is a large subject area so 940.5 can be subdivided again to cover the main historical events which have taken place in Europe throughout the 20th century:

940.53: the history of World War Two
940.54: the military history of World War Two
940.55: the history of Europe since 1945

So if you were studying a 20th century GCSE course and you wanted to find details about the D-Day Landings in 1944 you would look for a book with a classification number on its spine of 940.54:

900: history
940: European history
940.5: European history in the 20th century
940.54: the military history of World War Two

Of course you may need to use more than one book under the same classification in order to find all the details you need. So if you wanted to find more details on our previous example of Goering's involvement with 'Crystal Night' you could look at books with the number 940.5 (European history in the 20th century); 943 (the German section of European history); 920 (biography, where you could look up the life history of Goering).

Below is a list of Dewey classification numbers which you may find useful during the course of your studies. Remember these numbers can be subdivided even further in order to provide a more detailed and accurate description of the subject matter of the book.

355: military history
391: costume

560: prehistoric life e.g. fossils, dinosaurs etc
720: architecture
728: castles
932: Ancient Egypt
937: Ancient Rome
938: Ancient Greece
940.3/4: World War One
940.53/54: World War Two

The catalogue

All books in the library can be found in the library catalogue.

The catalogue could be a **cabinet** containing a number of drawers which house index cards for all the books in the library. The same information can be found in larger libraries on a computer terminal or **micro-fiche**.

A library catalogue is useful to you in your research in two ways. Imagine you are searching for more detailed information about our example. You do not know which books contain information about Field Marshal Goering's involvement with 'Crystal Night' so you would need to go to the **subject index** and find the subject title. (In this case it may appear under 'G' for Goering or 'R' for Reich Marshal.) These subject cards are stored in alphabetical order. If you found a card or other reference it would look something like this:

'Goering. Herman; German History: 943.086.'

The card tells you the Dewey classification number for the books dealing with this subject. You would then look up this number in the **classified** catalogue which will give you all the titles of the books in that particular library which contain information about Goering.

```
                                           943.086 090 4

AUTHORS NAME: . . . . Mosely. L

TITLE: . . . . 'The Reich Marshal'

PUBLISHER: . . . . Weidenfeld & Nicolson.
YR. of PUBLICATION: . . . . 1974
```

Having found the card and read all the information on it you could then find this particular book on the shelf marked with the same classification number.

The other way in which a library catalogue can be useful to you is if you already know that L. Mosely has written a book about Goering and you want to see if the library has it.

You would look at all the cards under Mosely.L in the **authors** catalogue and find the card containing the information about the subject you require. The card will be an exact copy of our previous example which we found in the classified catalogue. All cards in the authors catalogue are stored in alphabetical order according to the **surname**.

To summarize: you would use the same routine when searching for any non-fiction book you wish to see. If you know the **author's name**, find the relevant card, and therefore the classification number in the **authors index**. If, however, you only know the subject, find the card referring to that subject in the **subject index**, note the **Dewey number** then look for the card/cards with this same number in the **classified catalogue**. You will then find information on all the books in the library dealing with this subject. Once you have the number for the books you find them on the shelf with the same number.

Computer-controlled classification

It is important to note that some large libraries no longer use the Dewey system but have developed their own classification based on a computer program which is possibly linked to terminals in other libraries. In this way they can locate a book in any library in the area in a matter of seconds. Therefore if you do any research, or need to find a specific book in a library which does not seem to be using Dewey, ask the librarians at the desk to help you. If they have not got your book, they can give you a location of a copy by using the computer.

Using the book

Having found the book, how do you know it will be suitable for your research? The fact that the book is listed in the subject index, or catalogue, under the headings you were using suggests that it must contain some of the information you require. But some books contain many pages and a great deal of information, so how do you know, even if it has the correct title, that the book you have chosen contains suitable information for your project?

Using an index can save time.

First you can read the publisher's information contained on the **fly-leaf** of the book or the dust jacket. This, together with the **preface** at the very beginning of the book will usually give you a brief summary of its contents.

Another way is to look at the **chapter headings** on the **contents** page. It is possible to find out a great deal about a book by simply reading these pages. You should do this when you first pick up the book because it could save you a lot of time.

When you know the book is suitable, how do you find the details you need without having to read it all? All you need do is consult the index at the back of the book. Most non-fiction books have one. Each person, place, fact or subject mentioned in the book is listed in alphabetical order with its relevant page number informing the reader where the information can be found. e.g.

Cistercian Order. 89,91,92
Clerke,Clement. 169
Clocks: alarm,129,132; mechanical,
    128,130,132; pendulum, 136–7;
    portable, 133; spring-driven, 133–7,140;
    striking, 131,133; water, 128
Cloth production, 93,194
Clothing, trends in, 156,161 (*see also* Fashion)

You can see from this example that some of the entries in the list are subdivided into more references. If you were interested in clocks you could refer to individual types on the page references given. You would not necessarily have to read all the information on clocks.

Notice that the index may guide you to other references. In this example other information about 'trends in clothing' can also be found under 'fashion'. If you then look up fashion in the index you will find other page numbers dealing with this topic.

Other sources

We have dealt primarily with the use of books as a secondary source, but it must be remembered that there are other examples such as newspapers, magazines, maps, plans, etc which you may use during your course.

As with all secondary sources you must treat all of these sources on their merits and be aware of possible bias or influence.

Primary sources

You are more likely to use secondary rather than primary source material in your local study. However, if you have time or the opportunity, it may be useful to use some primary evidence. This can be found at home in the form of family photographs, or personal documents, medals, trophies etc, but there are many other types of documents and records which can be useful to the historian which are usually stored in the **local record office** (LRO). These can be **maps**, **census material**, **financial records**, **wills**, **inventories**, **school log books** and others. The LRO will probably be situated in your county town.

Each LRO in the country will have its own system of retrieving material and you will be told how to find the references to a particular document when you arrive at the office. However, there are some important things to remember when using any LRO:

Do not visit a record office without first telephoning and reserving a table.

1 Always telephone before you visit, to make sure they have an example of the document you wish to see. They will also reserve a table for you to work on.

2 Remember, record offices are very popular so *do not turn up without reserving your place!*

3 Archivists are very busy. They will give you advice on how to find the references to the documents you require but they will not have time to do the searching for you. So listen very carefully to the instructions they give you.

4 You will only be allowed to use a pencil to write with. So make sure you have one with you.

5 If you are examining census material be prepared for a long search.

6 If you want to trace any detail from a map you must ask at the desk for a piece of plastic to lay over the document in order to protect it.

7 Each LRO has rules and regulations, especially about coats and bags; so read them.

8 Do not disturb the other researchers.

9 Some documents can be photocopied, but not usually immediately. Beware, this can sometimes be expensive! Check the cost before you proceed.

If you follow all the instructions of the archivist and obey the rules and regulations, a visit to the record office can be both rewarding and fun.

You do not have to rely only on documents as primary source material. If you are doing a **local study** or **family project** an interview can provide you with a great deal of useful information, especially if you take a lot of care with the wording of the questions. It is important that they should be related to the topic. People will not wish to waste time answering questions which are irrelevant. It would be a good idea to show your proposed questions to your teacher before you use them.

Only interview people you have previously contacted. This can be done by letter or by telephone. You need to tell them why you want the interview and how it will form part of your individual study. The actual interview could be carried out over the telephone but do not forget that you need to obtain their permission to use their answers in your project.

The simplest way to record details from an interview is to use a tape-recorder, but again you must ask permission to use one before you start the interview because some people may object.

Important: If you have to go somewhere to interview a person always go with a friend or a member of your family. **Never go alone**!

If you require photographic evidence for your study you may have to do a lot of searching! Some local collections may be held at the LRO or the nearest museum but you will be lucky to find exactly what you need. Recent photographs of a local area might be obtained from the offices of the nearest local newspaper. You would need to contact them, giving a detailed description of what you need, and seek their permission to use relevant examples in your project.

It would be easier and more convenient to take modern photographs of a study area yourself. In this way you can determine the exact subject matter.

Checklist

1 Most history books contain secondary source material. A secondary source is one which has been produced later than the actual event or period being studied.

2 A primary source is one which remains in its original form, or has been produced during the actual time of the event or period in question.

3 A history book is the author's interpretation of the facts. Therefore history books can be biased.

4 If you have time it is always worth 'reading around' a topic before looking at a specialized book on the subject.

5 Biographies and autobiographies can be a useful source of information, but remember they can also be biased.

6 Historical novels, although sometimes enjoyable to read as stories, are of little use to you as a serious historian because they contain few historical facts.

7 Encyclopaedias and dictionaries can be found in the general reference section of a library.

8 Reference books such as these can provide you with limited, general information which can usually be found quickly. All the facts are listed in alphabetical order.

9 Multi-volume reference books may have a separate index volume listing all the subjects. This will also indicate the volume number and page in that volume on which the subject can be found.

10 Non-fiction books are stored on the shelves according to subject.

11 Non-fiction books are usually classified using the Dewey Decimal System.

12 History books are found between the numbers 900–999, but other information can be found in different sections.

13 **Note**: Some large libraries have developed their own cataloguing systems on a computer program which is compatible with computer terminals in other branch libraries. If this is the case in your library, ask the librarian for assistance.

14 All the books contained in a library can be found by using the catalogue.

15 You can find the information, contained either on file cards, microfiche or computer terminal in two ways:

● If you know the subject, but not the author, you would search in the subject index. The card/entry would give you the Dewey/reference number and you would then find an entry with this number in the classified catalogue.

- If you know the author and wish to know which books, written by him/her, are available in the library, you would find the information on the entries in the authors index under the author's surname.

16 There are two ways in which you can find out whether or not a book is suitable for your research:

- Read through the contents pages at the beginning of the book.

- Read the information written on the fly-leaf of the book, or in the preface.

Both ways can save you a lot of time.

17 To find the reference to individual facts you would need to consult the index at the back of the book, where the page numbers for all the people, places and events mentioned in the text of the book can be found.

18 Remember there are other secondary sources other than those in the written form. They should all be treated with the same care.

19 Always ring your Record Office before you go to make sure they have an example of the document you wish to see, and to reserve a desk.

20 You will only be allowed to use a pencil.

21 Listen carefully to instructions. The archivist will not find the references to documents for you.

22 Always work quietly. Do not disturb the other researchers.

23 Primary resource material can be obtained from an interview.

24 Remember to think very carefully about the questions before any interview.

25 If you have to go somewhere to interview a person **never** go alone.

26 It is convenient to tape-record an interview, but obtain permission *first*.

Use of evidence

In many of your GCSE assignments you will be given source material in the form of photographic evidence, written documents or cartoons.

Remember they are not there for illustration purposes, they are sources to provide you with information to use in your assignment answers. They should be treated very seriously. There are skills you need to know in order to use these sources effectively. Some of these skills are relevant to all source material but each has its own specific requirements which need identification. We will examine these in turn.

Photographs

Photographs, like all source material in an assignment, will be related to the topic in question. But how useful are they and what should you ask yourself about them?

There are two basic questions you should ask about any photographic evidence:

- What does the photographer want me to see in this picture? i.e. **witting testimony**.

- What else can I see in the picture that may be useful to me in answering the assignment question? i.e. **the unwitting testimony**.

Unwitting testimony can be extremely useful and can provide you with detailed information about the subject. It can often be more useful than the witting testimony as can be seen in our example below.

Examine Figure 10.1. This was taken in the 1920s and shows a machine which was used to dry the ink onto tinplate which was then made into biscuit tins. If this was given to you as a source in an assignment dealing with factory conditions how could it be used?

Question

What evidence is there in source 1 to suggest that little attention was paid to 'Health and Safety' in the 1920s?

The witting testimony is 'The drying machine'. However, it is the unwitting testimony in this photograph which provides us with the evidence to answer this question.

(a) These people are handling very sharp tinplate yet how many of them are wearing gloves?

(b) The lady in the centre of the picture is having to stand on a box in order to reach over the machine. Not only could her hand be cut by placing the tin into the dryer, but also her overall could be caught in the machinery. She also has heels on her shoes!

(c) Open, working machinery is within easy and dangerous reach of the workers and they could easily walk into the belts driving the machines.

(d) The drying racks at the side are open.

Fig. 10.1 This machine was used to dry ink onto tinplate

(e) There are tins and boxes lying on the floor where people could trip over them, etc . . .

These were not things that were taken by the photographer on purpose. But they do provide you with significant evidence to support your answer.

Having seen how useful photographs can be, what do you need to be wary of when using them? How do you know, for instance, that the photograph in the assignment is a genuine one?

Are all your photographs genuine or accurate?

Photographs, like any other source, can be biased. Not only can a photographic negative be 'adapted' at the processing stage but the photographer can select areas of the picture to be printed. Therefore the photograph may not give you an indication of what was in the original picture. Remember also that early photographs were **staged**. Plate cameras were used which required everybody to stand still.

At the turn of the century cameras were still rare. It is often the case that everybody in the picture was looking at the camera because they had never seen one before. Evidence of this kind in the photograph could give you a rough idea of how old it is. (Cameras were not invented until the 1840s.)

Another test of authenticity is to work out where the photographer was standing to take the picture, especially when you are given photographs of the First World War. Most of the genuine ones show troops attacking 'away' from the camera. Those with the troops coming towards the camera were often staged for propaganda purposes, so look out for them. They could still be useful as unwitting testimony but they provide little witting testimony. Do not take any photograph at face value. It must be treated as an important, but possibly biased source.

Written documents

The written documentary evidence you will see in your source material will come in many forms from simple recollections by an individual to extracts from government papers.

In your assignments you should be given the source of the material, or who a quote is attributed to. Take note of this and be very careful when reading source material written by an individual. Extracts from letters, diaries, journals and eye-witness accounts are the interpretation of the facts **by the person who experienced the event**. Although they can be very interesting and provide detail through the eyes and experience of an individual, the description can be very biased and can be affected by how the writer was feeling at the time. Some diarists used their writings to dispose of their anger or annoyance about something. Today this could give us an unbalanced view of what actually happened.

> *Eye witness accounts can be influenced by the persons emotions at the time. Therefore they can be biased.*

Letters were meant to be read by the person receiving them so they too can be biased, but they can provide some interesting unwitting testimony. Remember that most mail from war zones was **censored** so examples of these letters may only provide the 'official' version of the facts.

Government and personal documents should also be treated with care. Government departments are not above making mistakes and just because the source looks official it does not mean that it is reliable and totally accurate.

Cartoons

You may be given a cartoon as one of your sources. These usually depict a political or national event and can either contain a serious message or be humorous.

To use them effectively you need to examine them very carefully. First, read all the text and the caption. This may be at the bottom of the cartoon or in the form of speech coming from the characters. This can provide you with useful information. The date the cartoon was drawn and its source should also provide useful clues. Remember that if it comes from a newspaper the 'message' in the cartoon will be influenced by the political point of view of the newspaper.

Look at the cartoon characters; who do they depict?

Look very carefully for any other illustrated information that can be found in the picture: maps, uniforms, etc which could be of use to you.

Beware! Cartoons, like any other source can be biased and should be treated and examined with care.

Examine Figure 10.2. This is a cartoon by **Low** who was famous for his work in the Second World War. This example was in fact drawn in 1939 and depicts the Nazi-Soviet Pact.

In 1939 the only country which could stop Germany from seizing Poland was Russia. Stalin had been trying to secure an alliance with France and Britain but, at the time, both countries refused to have anything to do with communist Russia. In desperation Stalin signed a **non-aggression pact** with Hitler and both countries agreed not to attack each other. This Nazi-Soviet pact also contained secret clauses agreeing to divide Poland up between them after the invasion.

With this background knowledge the cartoon is easier to interpret.

- The two characters in the cartoon are obviously Hitler and Stalin. They are calling each other names because they both hated each other and the pact was really only for convenience.

- Hitler wanted no opposition to his invasion of Poland and Stalin did not want to have to go to war against Germany.

Fig. 10.2
A cartoon by Low

- The body lying between them represents Poland and the black clouds given an indication of a storm approaching, in this case the Second World War.

Other types of cartoon can refer to specific incidents which although serious were written in a humourous way. Figure 10.3 was drawn for *Punch* in 1917. It had always been a 'moan' of the common soldier that generals commanding the armies were rarely seen in the front line.

The final line in this dialogue is referring to that, i.e. the only time a general is seen is during a practice and never in the real thing!

Major-General (addressing the men before practising an attack behind the lines): 'I want you to understand that there is a difference between a rehearsal and the real thing. There are three essential differences: first, the absence of the enemy. Now *(turning to the Regimental Sergeant-Major)* what is the second difference?'
Sergeant-Major: 'The absence of the General, Sir.'

Cartoon in *Punch*, February 1917

Fig. 10.3 A cartoon from *Punch*

Posters have always played an important role in the field of **propaganda** and you are likely to see some of these as source material. They all contain a message, but you must remember that these can be very biased.

If you look at the three examples below you can see two different types. Figures 10.4 and 10.5 are very famous and were used to 'persuade' men to

Fig. 10.4 Lord Kitchener

Fig. 10.5 Emotions?

join the army. Figure 10.4 has a direct message, that Lord Kitchener, depicted on the poster, wants **YOU**, the reader of the poster, to join the army.

Figure 10.5 uses a different technique in order to put over the same message. It plays upon the emotions and the fact that the men's wives, girlfriends, daughters etc expect them to join the army and they would be doing themselves a disservice by not enlisting.

Figure 10.6 is a direct attempt to discredit the enemy and spread false stories and rumour. The German nurse is seen pouring water on the ground in front of a wounded soldier. The message clearly states that no British woman would ever think of doing such a thing and that any such action by the enemy would not be forgotten.

Fig. 10.6 Propaganda?

If you see examples of German propaganda posters drawn at the same time you will be aware that they carry the same messages from the German point of view. Posters were a legitimate part of propaganda warfare.

Statistics

You may see graphs or charts or other representations of statistics in your assignments. You know how to read line graphs and bar-charts in maths. Historical ones are used in the same way. However, it is very important to read the **labels** on the axes and the **title** of the graph.

It is also worth remembering when interpreting any statistical diagram that the information can be represented in a misleading way in order to support a specific theory or answer.

Always take note of any statistics.

Important facts can be omitted to make a graph or diagram biased towards one particular set of figures. Therefore it is useful to find out the source of the information whenever possible.

There is a useful book by D. Huff called *How to lie with Statistics*, published by Penguin, which is well worth reading. It explains in simple terms what to be aware of when using statistics.

All source material in your assignments should be treated with care. During your course your teacher will give you plenty of practice in identifying the useful detail contained in them. Remember however that they are not in the assignment just for decoration; they have to be used and referred to, especially when a question specifies the source to be used.

 **Checklist**

1 All source material contains some degree of bias so be wary of this.

2 Remember photographs can be 'adapted' to suit the need of the photographer. Sections can be processed from the negative to provide a different interpretation than that shown in the complete scene. So think very carefully about how, why and where the picture was taken. Could it be a fake?

3 Unwitting testimony in photographs, diaries and letters can be very useful.

4 Any source material written by individuals is their interpretation of the event and therefore can be biased. The account may have to be balanced by using other sources in the assignment or by information you have gathered during the course.

5 Just because a question specifies a source to be used it does not mean that you cannot use any of the others to support your answer.

6 Note the source of any historical cartoon. It may influence the message contained in it.

7 Statistics can be changed very easily to show a biased opinion. Note their source!

Glossary

Analyse To examine critically, part by part.

Annotation A written note/label on a diagram.

Archives Place in which public/historical records, charts, documents are stored and preserved.

Assignment A piece of work that has been alloted to a person/group of people.

Autobiography The life-story of an individual written by himelf or herself.

Biography The life-story of an individual written by someone else.

Concept An abstract notion. There are three main concepts in GCSE history:
- continuity and change
- similarity and difference
- cause and consequence.

Criteria Standards by which something is judged or assessed.

Cumulative Accumulating over a period of time.

Deploy To spread out.

Empathy An awareness of the ways in which other people and societies differ from your own. To identify with an historical situation as it appeared at the time of its occurrence and as experienced by those who were actually there.

Hypothesis A starting point or theory used as a basis from which to draw conclusions.

Index A table/chart to ease the finding of references in a book.

Integral An essential part of a whole.

Inventory A detailed list of articles making up the contents of a house etc.

Moderator One who acts as an arbitrator. One who judges the marks of a piece of work in conjunction with other similar examples.

Objective An aim/purpose.

Record office A local/county/national repository of documents.

Syllabus Outline or programme of topics as part of a course.

APPENDIX

Syllabus analysis

Exam Group	% Course-work	No. of Assignments	Word limit per Assignment	Total word limit		Assessment objectives
LEAG SYLLABUS A–C	30	3	–	4000	1	Evaluation of historical evidence
					2	Use of analytical concepts
					3	Empathy
MEG	30	4	–	2000–4500	1	Selection; deployment; communication
					2	Understanding basic concepts
					3	Empathy
					4	Use of evidence
NEA SYLLABUS A	40	4–7	–	6000		As syllabus B and C plus
					4	Interpretation of current situation in context of past
					5	Personal investigation. Description of site
					6	Relationship of site to its historical context
					7	Analysis of the role of the individual in history
NEA SYLLABUS B–C	30	4–6	–	3000–6000	1	Collection and collation of information
					2	Interpretation and evaluation of evidence
					3	Empathy
					4	Understanding basic concepts
SEG	20	2	1000	2000	1	Empathy
					2	Use of evidence
NIEC	20	3	750	2500	1	Selection; deployment; communication
					2	Understanding basic concepts, reliability of evidence
					3	Local study: (a) empathy
						(b) use of evidence
WEB	10	3	–	–	1	Use of evidence
					2	Empathy
					3	Causal relationship between past and present
	15	Extended essay + oral		1500	1	To Evaluate and select relevant knowledge
					2	Understanding basic concepts
					3	Display historical research skills
					4	Analyse and synthesize historical information

Examination groups: addresses

LEAG–London and East Anglian Group

London   University of London Schools Examinations Board
Stewart House, 32 Russell Square, London WC1B 5DN

LREB   London Regional Examinations Board
Lyon House, 104 Wandsworth High Street, London SW18 4LF

EAEB   East Anglian Examinations Board
The Lindens, Lexden Road, Colchester, Essex CO3 3RL (0206 549595)

MEG–Midlands Examining Group

Cambridge   University of Cambridge Local Examinations Syndicate
Syndicate Buildings, 1 Hills Road, Cambridge CB1 2EU (0223 61111)

O & C   Oxford and Cambridge Schools Examinations Board
10 Trumpington Street, Cambridge CB2 1QB and Elsfield Way, Oxford OX2 8EP

SUJB   Southern Universities' Joint Board for School Examinations
Cotham Road, Bristol BS6 6DD

WMEB   West Midlands Examinations Board
Norfolk House, Smallbrook Queensway, Birmingham B5 4NJ

EMREB   East Midland Regional Examinations Board
Robins Wood House, Robins Wood Road, Aspley, Nottingham NG8 3NR

NEA–Northern Examination Association (*write to your local board.*)

JMB   Joint Matriculation Board (061-273 2565)
Devas Street, Manchester M15 6EU (*also for centres outside the NEA area*)

ALSEB   Associated Lancashire Schools Examining Board
12 Harter Street, Manchester M1 6HL

NREB   North Regional Examinations Board
Wheatfield Road, Westerhope, Newcastle upon Tyne NE5 5JZ

NWREB   North-West Regional Examinations Board
Orbit House, Albert Street, Eccles, Manchester M30 0WL

YHREB   Yorkshire and Humberside Regional Examinations Board
Harrogate Office—31–33 Springfield Avenue, Harrogate HG1 2HW
Sheffield Office—Scarsdale House, 136 Derbyshire Lane, Sheffield S8 8SE

NISEC–Northern Ireland

NISEC   Northern Ireland Schools Examinations Council
Beechill House, 42 Beechill Road, Belfast BT8 4RS (0232 704666)

SEB–Scotland

SEB   Scottish Examinations Board
Ironmills Road, Dalkeith, Midlothian EH22 1BR (031-663 6601)

SEG–Southern Examining Group

AEB   The Associated Examining Board
Stag Hill House, Guildford, Surrey GU2 5XJ (0483 503123)

Oxford   Oxford Delegacy of Local Examinations
Ewert Place, Summertown, Oxford OX2 7BZ

SREB   Southern Regional Examinations Board
Eastleigh House, Market Street, Eastleigh, Hampshire SO5 4SW

SEREB   South-East Regional Examinations Board
Beloe House, 2–10 Mount Ephraim Road, Tunbridge Wells TN1 1EU

SWEB   South-Western Examinations Board
23–29 Marsh Street, Bristol BS1 4BP

WJEC–Wales

WJEC   Welsh Joint Education Committee
245 Western Avenue, Cardiff CF5 2YX (0222 561231)

(The boards to which you should write are underlined in each case.)

Coursework requirements

There now follows a detailed explanation of each examination group's requirements for coursework.

You may find some of the words used in the following descriptions a little confusing but most are explained in the glossary. However, it would be worthwhile reading the section relevant to you—i.e. the group whose examination you have been entered for—with your parents or teacher, so that you fully understand the requirements.

London and East Anglian Group (LEAG)

(Syllabus A, B and C)
Coursework will consist of three assignments with a maximum of 1500 words for each and will make up 30% of the total mark. The total amount of words used must not be more than 4000.

The objectives of the coursework will be to test:

1 The evaluation and interpretation of historical evidence:

Candidates will be expected to acquire the skills necessary for the study of various types of evidence. They will need to:

(a) understand evidence and place it in its historical context

(b) analyse, detect bias and identify gaps and weaknesses in the evidence

(c) interpret and evaluate evidence

(d) compare sources and reach conclusions based on the evidence

(e) show the ability to use all types of evidence.

2 The use of analytical concepts

Candidates will be expected to construct a simple, clear and coherent historical exposition using concepts such as:

(a) causation and consequence

(b) continuity and change

(c) similarity and difference

(d) the significance of an individual, movement or institution.

3 The ability to look at events and issues from the perspective of people in the past

Although the assignments will normally be written, one of the three may be totally, or in part, a computer program, piece of dramatic reconstruction, an historical model, debate or simulation.

LEAG Syllabus 'D'

Coursework will consist of between four and seven assignments and will comprise 40% of the total mark.

Parts of the syllabus to be assessed by coursework will be: the **Modern World** (15%), an **enquiry in depth** (10%) and a **local study** (15%).

Midland Examining Group (MEG)

Coursework will consist of four pieces of work, the overall word limit to be between 2000–4500 words. Will comprise 30% of total mark.

Assessment objective 1 The selection, deployment and communication of content.

Assessment objective 2 Understanding of basic concepts involved.

Assessment objective 3 Ability to place the chosen problem in context and to reveal an empathetic understanding of individuals and situations.

Assessment objective 4 Interpretation, use and evaluation of sources; relevance of conclusions drawn from the evidence provided in a number of sources.

Candidates may produce work on any topic drawn from, or closely related to, syllabus content.

Northern Examination Association NEA

Syllabus A

Coursework will comprise 40% of the total marks. Maximum word allowance: 6000.

Assessment objectives: (general)

1 The evaluation and interpretation of source material

2 A reconstruction of the ways of thinking and feeling of different persons in the past (empathy)

3 The analysis of causation and motivation

Specific objectives

4 An interpretation of the current situation in the context of past events (a study of the Modern World)

5 A personal investigation and description of a site ('History Around Us')

6 The relation of a site to its historical context ('History Around Us')

7 The analysis of the role of the individual in history (an enquiry in depth)

In order to gain maximum marks a candidate must do a minimum of four and a maximum of seven pieces of work which test **all** the objectives (1–7).

Assignments

Modern World 1 or 2 assignments 1250–2000 words. 10% of total marks.

Enquiry in depth 1 or 2 assignments 1250–2000 words. 10% of total marks.

History around us 2 or 3 assignments 2000–3000 words. 20% of total marks.

Syllabus B

Coursework will comprise of 30% of total mark. Candidates should complete a minimum of four and a maximum of six pieces of coursework. Total words should be not less than 3000 if higher levels are to be achieved. However, no penalties will be incurred if the objectives are satisfied. Coursework assignments will be based on the themes of **colonialism** and **human rights**. (If you are entered for this group your teacher will tell you of the choice of topic available in both of these categories.)

Assessment objectives (They are the same for syllabuses B and C.)

1 To collect and collate information in relation to a particular historical problem or topic and present it in a clear and understandable way

2 To interpret and evaluate a variety of historical sources, including primary and secondary written sources, statistical and visual material, artefacts, textbooks and orally transmitted information, by distinguishing between fact, opinion and judgment and by detecting deficiences such as gaps, bias and inconsistencies

3 Reconstruct past events as seen from the perspectives of people in the past

4 Use historical information to demonstrate an understanding of the concepts of cause and consequence, continuity and change, similarity and difference.

The use of material, other than written, can be submitted providing it has sufficient written explanation.

Syllabus C

Coursework will carry 30% of the total mark. Candidates must attempt a minimum of four and a maximum of six pieces of work testing all the assessment objectives. (See syllabus B.)

Words allowance as in Syllabus B.

At least one assignment must be based on each of the three themes of the syllabus:

- industrialization and urbanization
- responses to industrialization
- social improvements

At least one assignment must be based on the local aspects of one of the three themes.

Your teacher will tell you of the choice of topics available within each broad theme. As in syllabus B your work can be submitted in a form other than written but it must be explained.

Northern Ireland Examinations Council

Coursework will consist of three common assignments and will comprise 20% of the total mark.

Candidates must:

(a) show their ability to undertake an historical enquiry

(b) develop historical reasoning

(c) express their knowledge and understanding through local study:

- study of a site
- study of an event
- study of an individual, family or community
- local agriculture, industry, transport or education.

The study must concentrate on the Ulster connection and its bearing on the impact within the context of Ulster, but may relate to the wider world.

Assignment 1 (750–1000 words)
Candidates should show their ability to:
undertake an historical study, communicate historical knowledge in a sequential narrative, recall and select knowledge relevant to the study.

Candidates should comment on the range of sources used and credit will be given to those finding and using evidence other than that given to them by their teacher.

Assignment 2 (500–750 words)
Will test candidates' historical understanding and reasoning related to two assessment objectives:

(a) cause/consequence, continuity/change, similarity/difference

(Should be presented as continuous prose though relevant diagrams, drawings and photographs can be included.)

(b) reliability of evidence.

Assignment 3 (500–750 words)

(a) Use a local study to demonstrate an ability to look at events and issues from the perspective of people in the past.

(b) An analysis of various types of historical evidence and the ability to reach conclusions based on their comparisons.

Southern Examining Group (SEG)

Paper 3 Coursework

Will consist of two written assignments, each of which must not exceed 1000 words and comprise 20% of the total mark.

Assignment 1 Must be primarily concerned with assessment objective 3: looking at events and issues from the perspectives of people in the past (**empathy**).

Assignment 2 Must be primarily concerned with assessment objective 4: showing the skills necessary to study a wide variety of historical sources, such as primary and secondary written sources, statistical and visual material (including moving film, if appropriate), artefacts, textbooks and orally transmitted information. Candidates should demonstrate their skills of using the material by:

1 understanding and extracting information from it

2 distinguishing between fact, opinion and judgment, and indicating the deficiencies of the material as useful evidence, such as inconsistency of evidence and bias

3 comparing various types of historical sources and making conclusions based on this comparison.

Each piece of coursework should be directly related to a theme or topic within the syllabus. It must be the original work of the candidate. Assignments may take the form of structured exercises or written as an essay.

Each candidate's coursework must be kept in an individual file which will be kept safely locked away by your teacher.

Welsh Examining Board

Coursework will take the form of an extended essay, including an oral, and three written assignments. 25% of the final GCSE grade will be allocated to coursework of which 15% will be for the extended essay.

The extended essay will be restricted to a maximum of 1500 words. A choice of titles will be provided by the teacher.

The four aims of the essay are:

1 to, evaluate and select knowledge relevant to the subject; to analyse this knowledge and write it in a readable form

2 to make use of, and understand, the concepts of cause/consequence, change/continuity, similarity/difference

3 to show the skills necessary to do independent historical research and record the findings of that research

4 to analyse and synthesize historical information.

The three written assignments will be based on:

(a) an exercise requiring the use of evidence

(b) an exercise requiring empathy

(c) past/present exercise; a test of the understanding of the causal relationship between current and past events.

Schools history project

Coursework makes up 40% of final grade.
Offers four component parts:

1 A study in development: either medicine or energy. (This is examined by the group and is worth 20%)

2 A study in depth: one of the following: Elizabethan England, Britain 1815–51, The American West. 10% coursework (10% Exam).

3 Modern World: Topics can be chosen from a wide selection. 10% coursework.

4 History around us.

As you can see there are many different boards with many alternative aims and objectives. Therefore it must be stressed again that it is very important that you listen carefully to all the information and instructions about the particular examination group you are entered with. If you do not you could find yourself behind in the coursework.

Summary

A All GCSE groups require candidates to do coursework and at least 20% of the final mark will be gained from this coursework.

B Coursework is a very important part of GCSE and should be taken very seriously. The marks you earn could make a significant difference to your final grade.

C Your teacher will tell you the requirements of the group you are entered with so **listen very carefully**.

D The important requirements of some groups are as follows:

- **LEAG** (Syllabuses A, B and C) three assignments of 1500 words. 30%
- **LEAG** (Syllabus D) four to seven assignments. 40%
- **MEG** four assignments. Limit 2500–4500 words. 30%
- **NEA** (Syllabus A) between four and seven assignments. Total words 6000. Based on themes of Modern World, an enquiry in depth and history around us. 40%
- **NEA** (Syllabus B) four assignments based on the themes of colonialism and human rights. 30%
- **NEA** (Syllabus C) between four and six assignments based on industrialization, urbanization, responses to industrialization, social improvements. Total words; minimum of 300 to gain higher levels. 30%
- **NIEC** three assignments. Total limit 2500 words. 20%
- **SEG** two assignments of 1000 words each. 20%
- **WEB** extended essay, oral, three assignments. 25%

INDEX